UNLOCKING

THE

SCHOOLHOUSE

DOOR

ESSAYS ON THE MISUNDERSTANDINGS
OF PUBLIC EDUCATION

Larry White

Lucky Bat Books

A Lucky Bat Book

Unlocking the Schoolhouse Door:
Essays on the Misunderstandings of Public Education

Copyright 2016 by Larry White

Cover Design: Nuno Moreira

Published by Lucky Bat Books
LuckyBatBooks.com

10 9 8 7 6 5 4 3 2 1

ISBN: 978-1-943588-29-9

This book also available in digital formats.

CONTENTS

CONTENTS

CONTENTS

PREFACE

"Is this all there is?"

This is what I was asking myself when, after thirty-four years teaching high school, which included teaching at least ten different courses and coaching at least five different sports, I retired. I felt lost. During that first year of "retirement," I supervised new teachers, volunteered in elementary school classrooms, and tutored in after-school programs. I was just trying to stay present in the classroom.

I still felt as if a part of me were missing. I still had things to say, to teach. My educator voice, at least in my own mind, would not quit. So I wrote my ideas down. The document ended up being a six-thousand-word ramble.

Coincidentally, the daughter of my city's newspaper editor was a student in the class in which I volunteered. I made contact with him and asked him to look at the composition for me. He wanted to know whether I was interested in having the work published. If so, I needed to reduce the length by half and break it into four stories of about seven hundred fifty words.

That was my introduction to professional writing. From there, the editor suggested that I continue preparing articles on education. Although the original four essays dealt mainly with high school, subsequent essays delved into a wide variety of educational topics. It was somewhat like an addiction; I had found an outlet for my ideas and passion for the classroom.

My original impetus to put my thoughts on paper was the result of numerous conversations that had taken place over the decades with teachers, parents, and other members of the business community. There seemed to be gaps of understanding among the various groups' perspectives on the world of school.

Additionally, I was invited to make a presentation in 2010 to a local service club whose members were civic and community leaders, business owners and managers, attorneys, medical professionals, etc. They were respectful and appreciative of my ability to present and articulate responses. However, their questions and comments made it abundantly clear to me that the lens through which they viewed education was completely out of focus.

It became evident to me that although I could claim a zero degree of expertise in their professional endeavors, they had designated themselves experts on how to "fix" schools. These professionals seemed to be saying that because they had gone to school and received undergraduate and/or advanced degrees decades prior, they knew best how to deal with the educational system and its problems.

On one hand, it seemed to me that teachers themselves were viewing educational issues through the lens of classroom needs. This meant they saw a lack of resources, both personal and professional, as well as the overwhelming time and stress involved in helping their students succeed.

On the other hand, the members of the business community seemed to be viewing education through the lens of their own experience and memories of schooling from past decades, and whether they involved lectures, textbooks, rules for order, uniforms, etc. And they often expressed solutions that were unrealistic, such as "just kick those kids out of school" or "make their parents do their jobs."

Members of the non-education community often saw teachers as lazy, as if they were on welfare—receiving free handouts because they left school at three o'clock and had summers and holiday seasons off from work. And from their viewpoint, schools were failing.

My essays are an attempt to address these gaps in understanding. There is such an overwhelming degree of misunderstanding surrounding education that it makes it all the more difficult to arrive at effective solutions.

I hope your reading of these essays fosters reflection and discussion of the challenges schools and teachers face in trying to educate future generations of American citizens.

PART ONE

——————

THE BIG PICTURE:

THE REAL PURPOSE OF EDUCATION

ESSAY 1:

SEARCHING FOR THE PURPOSE

If you were to ask most successful adults today what they wanted to become when they were, say, sixteen years of age, I think more often than not they would either say they don't know or don't remember, or that they wanted to become something other than what they actually became.

So, then, if what people end up choosing for their careers is different from what they originally contemplated, how, exactly, were they supposed to have been trained in school to achieve their ultimate objectives? Was it textbook knowledge alone that has gotten them where they are?

If you ask most professional adults what they believe students should learn by the time they graduate high school, those adults often indicate that students need to know more about math, science, current events, or literature. Many people expect that students just need to know more, period. But as to how to quantify what learning is, our current methods fall short.

These sentiments often are echoed in the headlines that pre-dominate mass media today. Such headlines tout, "American students score among the lowest in the developing world," or, "U.S. students place 26th in science and math, and high school students not civic-minded." Some headlines even seem to suggest that Americans are illiterate.

These sentiments express the failures of, or at least the challenges met by, America's high schools and their students, both in the United States and abroad. These criticisms reflect an overall negative view of our students' achievement as compared to that of students from other countries. Therefore, according to these critics of our public education system, the United States is failing to prepare students for the future, not only in competitive fields in the twenty-first century, but for life in general.

With regard to students' abilities as reflected by scores on specific exams, on average, those critics often appear correct.

In response to these achievement scores, every interested party, from elected legislators and federal or state bureaucrats to teachers' unions and boards of education, has proposed solutions to address these deficiencies. Most of these solutions presume that students need to show they have stored more "stuff" in their heads—more data, formulas, dates, vocabulary.

These solutions demonstrate that we are missing a set of defined objectives regarding the value of a high school education—that of learning the skills necessary to function in the real world of LIFE. The real purpose of high school is to help students develop purpose as they head out into the world.

I would like to help generate discussion and debate between the general public and the educational community to promote an understanding of, and improvement in, the teaching and learning of students.

Over the last generation, the educational system, specifically at the high school level, has become overwhelmed by continuous and confusing directives regarding students' performance on tests and has lost its focus. In the past, schools were responsible for keeping order in the classroom through discipline and providing information that helped students to learn. The rest was left to the parents and the at-large community (extended family, neighbors, church members, community recreation centers, members of the general population, etc.); these people were charged with providing the relationships, values, and opportunities for application of useful knowledge. But today, schools are tasked with providing all of these things.

Also, as society has changed, schools, by extension, have been expected to provide meals, after-school programs, hearing and vision testing, expanded special education and resource services, security policing, drug testing, and more. Schools also are required, by order of politicians, to ensure that students be measured by how well they digest and regurgitate accumulated knowledge at will on state- and federally mandated assessments.

For those students who have not acquired the basic educational tools of our traditional three "R's" (readin', 'ritin', and 'rithmetic, of course), those skills become the primary focus of their teachers, as these skills are required in order to proceed successfully in the postsecondary and professional worlds. And there are many who lack these prerequisites.

However, significant numbers of students do possess the required knowledge and skills in abundance and enroll in honors, Advanced Placement, and International Baccalaureate-type courses. Most others can function effectively, even as they take a curriculum that may be designed to admit them into a community college, trade school, the military, or employment after high school.

What all students need, whether they choose to follow an academic route after high school or not, is what I call R.S.V.P.

R is for the relationships that students need to be able to develop with peers, employers, and their community.

S is for the subject-matter content that is truly fundamental for a discipline's framework.

V is for the values necessary for members of a civic democracy.

P is for the ability to process knowledge in a meaningful way.

The goal, then, is for schools to teach students to become respectful, caring, involved individuals who have developed the skills and capacity for thinking and learning in the world in which they will live.

ESSAY 2:

PURPOSEFUL BUILDING BLOCKS: RELATIONSHIPS AND VALUES

The ability to engage in positive, meaningful relationships with both peers and adults is a component often lacking in the lives of adolescents.

Whether it is because of lack of literacy, poverty, reliance on technology, family structure, or barriers in language or ethnicity, significant numbers of students lack the skills and competency necessary to compete effectively in the post-high school world.

And in this increasingly diverse world, the ability to relate to one another is crucial in terms of our roles as consumers, employees, citizens, and even members of Congress.

Our diversity does, in many ways, constitute one of America's greatest strengths. However, it also presents some tremendous challenges. Because we have vast differences among us, students find few cultural commonalities in their classrooms in terms of life experiences, parental roles, prior knowledge, and discipline among fellow students, so that there isn't really a common foundation.

Yet one central, unifying experience in which all members of our society engage and where these qualities can be acquired is high school, where increasingly disparate populations converge. School is where development of interpersonal relationships and promotion of common values can occur.

However, there are often misunderstandings regarding the application of these concepts. For example, the term "relationships" certainly does not mean that the goal is to have teachers become students' friends, although friendship may be a byproduct of their time spent together. Nor am I saying that teachers should become strict, rule-enforcing disciplinarians who are disconnected from their clientele.

What I mean by "relationships" is teaching students how to engage in a respectful, positive way that contributes to learning.

Also, in regard to "values," I am not suggesting that high schools and teachers present students with their personal perspectives on issues of political or religious correctness. Many suggest that it is the parents' place, not the schools', to teach values. Unfortunately, too often that does not occur, or it is done out of societal context.

Just as roles and relationships are vastly different across our ethnic mosaic, so are values. However, despite those differences, some fundamental values need to be shared among all members of our community.

For example, in order to have a literate and educated populace, schools need to promote and encourage civic participation, individual rights, tolerance, equality, and justice to achieve that objective. In other words, there are specific concepts or skills that need to be held in common.

Teachers are the individuals best situated to promote these objectives.

Most teachers work hard to establish useful and meaningful connections with students—connections that are necessary in order to better prepare students to become contributing members of society. These teachers treat students with respect and good manners and expect the same in return. They also work hard to make individual contact with each student every day.

Sadly, there are some students for whom this type of contact rarely occurs, at home or in schools. It is possible for a student to go through an entire day without ever being acknowledged by an adult, either positively or negatively. For some others, it is only the latter.

In order to formulate a core commonality of purpose in education, instruction in the promotion of relationships and values needs to extend beyond just teacher and student. Peer-to-peer communication through structured discussion and time for intrapersonal reflection are also necessary.

Teachers, too, need to know their students. Teachers should attempt to engage with students to understand the students' backgrounds, interests, and activities, as a way to get to know each one's unique characteristics. This enables teachers to tailor lessons, readings, and strategies more effectively to their students' needs and interests, which will help and encourage them to fulfill the objectives of the course while promoting the desired formation of relationships and values.

Many teachers do seek out these positive connections by making efforts to attend their students' out-of-class activities, such as sporting events; theater performances; and music, dance, or art exhibitions. These actions also work to solidify effective classroom behaviors.

However, in order to work toward a common objective of a better society for all, the ability to communicate respectfully with one another and cooperative effectively are necessary—but too often missing—objectives.

High school can help fill that void.

ESSAY 3:

EDUCATED LIVES MATTER

There are numerous concerns to be addressed in this country, from Black Lives Matter to LGBT Lives Matter, Immigrant Lives Matter, All Lives Matter, and innumerable others. But beneath all the labels are still the issues of how we as human beings and citizens of this country treat one another. In addition, we need to look at the basic concept of how individuals and society gain access to improvements in the human condition—the life, liberty, and pursuit of happiness that we all desire.

Underlying these objectives, I believe, is education and living an educated life. Education can ultimately be a game changer in terms of income, employment, health, individual and familial relationships, and societal improvement.

If you closely examine yourself and the community at large, you will see that educational level often dictates your connectivity to certain individuals and groups in society. The neighborhood in which you live probably contains individuals with similar educational attainment as you and relatively similar incomes.

I'm sure that the same can be said for the people with whom you work, attend church or clubs, and engage in activities. Education matters to you, and you probably made distinct choices to obtain it. I would wager that those of you who choose to read this column have attained a level of literacy that accompanies the definition of middle or upper class.

Moreover, the same can be said for those individuals on the opposite end of the spectrum. I would imagine that individuals with lower educational attainment can be assigned similar parameters. The less educated, whether white, black, brown, Christian, Muslim, Jewish, or atheist, are generally poor, live in less desirable neighborhoods, and work and associate with similarly educated friends. They often face greater degrees of health-related problems, larger numbers of single-parent families, and more incidents of crime and gang behaviors.

Poverty also matters, and that is often a result of illiteracy and lower educational attainment. However, poverty itself doesn't automatic point to illiteracy. Through the adjustment of priorities and with individual effort, education can still be acquired. But it requires that people make the right choices.

Often, the behaviors that lead to poverty are a result of poor choices. As I used to say to my students, there are two things that are guaranteed in life, and they are not death and taxes. They are death and choices. We all die at some point, and we cannot control the final result, but we can often control *how* we live until then.

The children of these poor and illiterate parents cannot control the choices that their parents made, but through education, we can help provide these children with the tools (knowledge and skills) they need to make smarter choices in the future to aid them in exiting poverty.

Every day we make a multitude of choices, from what to eat or wear to whom to hang around with and what behaviors in which to engage. Even choosing to do nothing is still a choice. The people who make the smartest choices are the ones most likely to find success. And choosing to be educated is one of those smart choices. Being educated doesn't necessarily mean acquiring a college degree, but that helps. It means becoming a lifelong learner with a passion to grow in knowledge and experience.

However, with every choice you make, you have to give something up. That is called an opportunity cost. If you choose to learn and study, whether it be for a math test, band practice, or an athletic endeavor, you are choosing to give up something else—perhaps video games, Facebook time, or hanging out with other poor decision-makers. For many, due to negative influences, those are challenging choices.

Society, too, has to make choices. These choices may be between protecting the environment or preventing potential loss of jobs in an industry, such as the coal industry; between providing military expenditures or funding health care; or between protecting individual liberties or ensuring national security. Thus, just like with individuals, the voters and their elected representatives give something up every time they choose one side of an issue over another. And, just like with individuals, those choices can be challenging as well.

Education provides the means by which individuals can work alone or as part of communities to effectively address problems and begin to research, discuss, and develop solutions. The smartest choice we can make is to assure that all people, particularly young people, acquire the educational opportunities necessary in order to play a part in making these improvements and solving those problems.

This may mean sacrificing some deeply held views on the role of government; on ways of dealing with health, poverty, and welfare; and on altering our concepts of schools and what schools do for their communities. But at the end of the day, a better school means a better society for us all.

That is why educated lives matter.

ESSAY 4:

MISUNDERSTANDING CONTENT

Think of learning as an obstacle course. Students must navigate over, under, and through a series of increasingly challenging obstacles. Each one must also carry an object while doing so: the content. The goal for students is to effectively maneuver through the course, not to carry a bigger weight. Once they have successfully acquired the skills necessary to traverse the obstacles, *then* they can add weight. Schools and teachers are often trying to pile on weight, yet they are not teaching students how to navigate the obstacles.

When students get lost in the obstacles, we lose them. We can't afford to lose them. Enough have been lost already.

This does not mean that teachers need to entertain students. We must engage their minds and bodies to participate, to create, to think, and to question—actively, not passively. The ability to make connections in understanding content—to see how points in the obstacle course connect—is what makes learning valuable. That is the real objective.

The content that students are supposed to memorize and regurgitate for state tests—formulas, procedures, dates, conjugations, and vocabulary—doesn't matter. Seriously, *these things do not matter* in terms of future success. Success in life is not measured by how well a person performs on tests.

In content terms, adults acquire a great deal of knowledge as they mature in their chosen fields. Much of this learning happened outside of school, and it was helped by the fact that the knowledge was called upon and used with regularity. Meanwhile, I am sure most can recall the drudgery of sitting in classes where information was presented in lecture or outline format, or from voluminous lists of vocabulary, only to be regurgitated for some test, yet they cannot remember the content. How does that demonstrate learning?

In too many high school classes, varying degrees of that drudgery still exist. Schools and teachers are missing the point.

Why? The reasons are many.

Teachers have a tendency to fall back on the way they themselves were taught. Sometimes, because of testing requirements, teachers feel they have to cram content into a limited time frame so students score better on multiple-choice exams.

In some cases, teachers use heavy content loads as a way to manage overwhelming numbers of students. Also, maybe that is the only delivery strategy a teacher has learned.

In any case, the result is the same. Students get bored, teachers get frustrated, and society loses.

This is not to say that having the basic building blocks of knowledge doesn't count. It certainly does. The quantity of content, however, doesn't matter as much as people think it does. And that is just the point.

Many students enter high school with substandard literacy skills. Basing education on a curriculum heavily laden with content is a waste of time and energy for both the teacher and student.

It makes a lot more sense to determine the competency level at which each student functions and establish a curricular challenge that meets that student's needs.

An interesting thing about content is that there is so much of it. Moreover, in today's Internet-based world, the quantities of knowledge that students have available at the touch of a button are almost limitless. And believe me, they have access to a lot of buttons. Students can also access information faster than most adults.

The point is that students do not need to be force fed subject matter.

Instead, they just need to learn how to contextualize and utilize content in meaningful ways. That is a significant component missing from many high school classrooms.

The purpose of high schools, then, is to train students in a concept I call "A.I.R." Every successful person in our society does this on a daily basis: Acquire information, Interpret information, Reprocess and present information. Doctors and lawyers, businessmen and journalists, auto mechanics and fast-food servers perform those three things every day. That is what we should be teaching students to do.

The teacher should provide the framework to facilitate A.I.R. through the use of content.

This facilitation should incorporate how to select topics for investigation or study, how to research and evaluate sources, and how to gather and organize material. Teachers should assist students in working with peers, discuss with students the information they've gathered, decide on which medium students should use (videos, PowerPoints, papers, skits, posters, activities, etc.) to convey the information, and help them to develop and present information.

Sure, content is definitely needed, but the *process* is what inculcates the learning.

ESSAY 5:

ACHIEVING OBJECTIVES

This is a time of great expectations in education. The challenges are many. The degree to which our educational system can address these challenges may dictate our future.

In the previous four essays, I attempted to introduce the purpose of today's high schools: R.S.V.P., which stands for developing Relationships, presenting Subject-matter content, teaching Values, and Processing information. Below are some changes that, if made in schools, could help them to achieve these objectives.

• *Class Size.* Size does matter. Teachers can and do adapt to changing circumstances. However, when numbers reach thirty-six to forty-two students per class, with extreme ranges among students' abilities and skills, the challenges in effectively reaching R.S.V.P. become overwhelming. The magnification of all variables exponentially magnifies the difficulty. As a result, teaching often becomes more about survival than learning.

• *Instructional Coaches.* Teachers, especially at the high school level, are a particularly isolated species. The classroom is their domain, and administrators generally visit classrooms once or twice a year for observation purposes. Teachers are often reluctant to discuss challenges for fear that doing so will result in negative evaluations. But most teachers would benefit from a second pair of eyes. They might also be willing to try out new strategies or activities in a more open, nonjudgmental atmosphere. Coaches could be of great assistance to them by facilitating discussion and reflection as well as providing insights and resources.

However, in the long run, after receiving this coaching, teachers need to be held accountable for effective teaching or encouraged to pursue new careers. Student education, the teaching professing, and societal advancement requires it.

• *Administrative support.* Many administrators have spent little time teaching or have not worked in classrooms for years. They themselves often have little training in the subject-matter content areas in which they supervise and are often unfamiliar with effective current strategies. In addition, they also have little time, since they have to deal with discipline, security, expulsions, and parent issues.

Campuses too frequently become settings for "us-versus-them" situations. Districts need to recognize that effective relationship development and coaching should extend to administrators as well, or they should be replaced.

• *Common Core.* Common Core standards need continued emphasis. Unfortunately, the understanding, communication, and implementation of these standards is fragmented, and Common Core is misunderstood by most segments of the community. Since education has been driven by massive high-stakes assessments for the last decade, many district officials, site administrators, and teachers have become dependent on methodologies meant only to achieve desired test results. The switch to Common Core will better prepare our students for their futures by teaching them to think.

• *Technology.* If the objective in education is to move from content loading to knowledge processing, the tools and services needed to conduct that work should be available. If we want students to become skilled with current resources, then those resources must be provided. For the most part, they are not. Schools need more computing hardware, updated software, and applicable training.

• *Parent Involvement.* Obviously, there are as many types of parenting behaviors as there are students. They range from the overly involved "helicopter parents" to the absentee variety, or worse, the harmful ones. However, most parents are as confused and concerned as everyone else about what effective strategies to employ in helping their teenagers succeed. Schools have been working hard to establish connections with parent groups. But stronger efforts should be applied, especially when it comes to holding parents accountable, along with their children, for poor attendance and misbehavior. Schools and communities need to provide parents with better education about what is required in order for their children to succeed.

• *Community Volunteers.* Today's schools are vastly different from those that existed in the 1950s and '60s. However, the adage, "It takes a village to raise a child," is truer today than ever before. It may not be feasible for parents and community volunteers to easily find their places in high schools today, but their places can be found in primary grades. Schools must encourage and train more parents and community members as tutors and classroom aides. Yes, that puts the onus on schools, which already have too much to do, but in many cases, parents are just not taking the responsibility to get involved by themselves. They need much more prompting and enticement to do so.

• *Money.* I realize that everything seems to come back to more money for education. However, there is such a lack of resources to accomplish the above suggestions that without more money, there will be negligible results. Sometimes it does come down to paying now or paying later. We have to consider our priorities. Schools need to work with business and community leaders to establish foundations, grants, and adopt-a-school programs to fund education.

By focusing stakeholders' attention on the missing objectives in high school education—away from the strict acquisition of content and toward the development of effective relationships, the promotion of values, and the effective processing of information, we can reignite the purpose of school in the minds of our students, and we can preserve our future as well. Please R.S.V.P.

PART TWO:

_____

INSIGHTS INTO THE WORLD OF SCHOOL

ESSAY 6:

THE PARENT TRAP

A student kicks his teacher and then repeats the same behavior after being brought to the counselor.

Another student is brought to the principal because of constant class disruption. During the conference with the principal, the student throws all of the items on the principal's desk, including the hot cup of coffee, onto the floor.

During class, a separate student cusses out the teacher, in front of classmates, after being caught stealing.

On a regular basis, another student misses school or is marked tardy an average of one day a week.

Our last student, even after ongoing communication from the teacher, fails to complete or submit homework on nine out of ten days.

These stories reflect inappropriate student behaviors that are not tolerated in today's high schools. However, these scenarios are not taken from a high school ledger or even from a middle school. These are stories of elementary school students, in grades kindergarten through third.

In many ways, these students are handicapped, and significantly so. However, their handicaps are not physical or cognitive. They are parental.

More often than not, the challenges children face result from absentee or negative parenting, by people who by and large never acquired adequate levels of education themselves and lack the capacity or energy to properly raise their children.

As a result of these handicaps, by the time these students reach high school, they are two to five grade levels behind where they should be, often in both language and math. To an even greater degree, these students are handicapped in attitude, maturity, and responsibility.

These are the students who fail to graduate high school, enroll in college, find meaningful employment, and contribute as citizens. Then, too often, they repeat the process of producing and rearing uneducated children.

These parents come in all shapes and sizes, all races and ethnicities, and all language origins. The one thing they have in common is they are not effective parents.

All too often, they pass along the responsibility of rearing their children to schools. Then these same parents blame the schools for not fostering the students' growth to acceptable levels in terms of test scores, grades, or behaviors, and they raise hell if their children are caught or blamed for any negative actions and are consequently punished.

This issue is too frequently the unspoken cause of our educational ills, and it is the most pervasive. Trying to ensure the educational attainment of these students is something akin to trying to raise a hot air balloon that is filled with holes before it leaves the launch. This gas heap is not going to fly.

The prime, but not only, reason for this lack of parental efficacy is poverty. Poverty is both a cause and result of illiteracy, low educational attainment, or unemployment, and poverty is a contributing factor in gang activity, drug use, and crime. The issue of poverty is not something that schools can solve.

The most significant way that schools can help facilitate progress out of these circumstances is through education. However, this education cannot be the responsibility of schools alone.

Our citizens and politicians need to reevaluate their priorities and establish an affirmative action program for education.

This affirmative action does not involve placing a student's race, ethnicity, gender, or place of origin above another, but rather taking steps to prepare parents for the challenges they face in raising their children.

This action involves several directives, involving both a carrot and a stick.

First, schools should expand learning opportunities for parents by offering programs such as reading sessions, whereby teachers coach parents in reading with or to their children and following up with questions, or they help parents to better assist their children with understanding basic math operations. They could take place during teacher-parent conference sessions, which already occur one to four times a year. These conferences should also incorporate discussions on turning off the TV, providing nutritious foods, communicating with school personnel, and preparing budgets. These sessions should begin even before students start school. Teachers need to be compensated with additional prep time to conduct these activities.

Schools and communities should not only provide activities, events, and speakers that encourage parents to come to them, but they should consider methods for such learning opportunities to go to parents as well. Weekly gatherings should take place in the communities themselves, through social welfare departments, community hospitals, religious organizations, and the school system, beginning shortly after children are born.

Many parents have had negative experiences in schools and are wary of authority. Systems must be developed that encourage parents to overcome their resistance and become comfortable enough to get involved in their children's schooling.

Businesses and community and church organizations should be encouraged to participate by contributing funding or even expertise; after all, these individuals are future customers, clients, and citizens.

Finally, we must raise our expectations of parents who receive public assistance; they ought to be held accountable for performing their parental duties. If children are not attending or performing appropriately in schools, or if they are displaying behaviors disruptive to school, there ought to be incentives for their parents to work toward improving those situations, or they should forfeit some of that public assistance.

Raising a child truly does take a village, but the parents are an integral part of that village.

If we want to foster a better society, we all need to be prepared to act affirmatively in extending a hand. We also need to demand that people grab a hold of that hand.

ESSAY 7:

COMMON CORE, COMMON SENSE

To think or not to think. That is the core of the issue in education today. And in regard to that issue, common sense comprehension is also not so common, but misunderstanding is.

Over the last decade, K-12 education has been driven by No Child Left Behind (NCLB) legislation that was passed by Congress in 2001. One of the main purposes of the act was to provide disadvantaged students access to the basic skills needed for success. The idea was that these skills would be assessed through an annual test, and the results were to be used to promote a wide variety of reforms. These test results were made public, and schools were held accountable for growth. If growth did not proceed according to certain prescribed patterns, then districts, administrators, and teachers would have to make changes.

The challenge has been that the testing was so driven by recall of data and factoids that all the stakeholders involved, from students and parents to teachers, administrators, politicians, and business people have been asking for years, "So what? What does the score mean for this child's learning and for our society in general?" The knowledge did not translate into meaningful learning or applicable skills that students or anyone else could actually use.

Also, in many cases, teachers lost the ability to really teach. The textbook and rote learning became the driving force behind education. In many schools, teachers were required to read mandated instructions and follow prepared scripts for their lessons. Every teacher in a specific grade or subject was supposed to be on the same lesson, page, and assignment on the same day, and they were evaluated accordingly.

Textbook publishers loved the results, but students didn't. And they didn't learn—if by learning we mean possessing useful knowledge and employable skills needed to function effectively in today's world.

Now the pendulum in education has started swinging again. With Common Core State Standards, it is heading in the right direction, if we can achieve our target and stay there.

The purpose of Common Core is to teach the *how* and *why* of knowledge, not just the *what*. That is going to be a challenge. With NCLB, the "what" of teaching and learning was easy to identify. Learning specific subject-matter content data (vocabulary, dates, names, formulas, procedures, etc.) was supposed to be simply a matter of input and output.

With the Common Core Standards, learning may not be quite so easy, but it will certainly be more valuable. Education will emphasize the *process* of teaching and learning. The old adage, "Inquiring minds want to know," will become the mantra for which education strives and one which society demands.

Students will still be tasked with acquiring subject-matter content but also with being able to *do* something with that knowledge—something that will be authentic and useful in the real world. This something might be to access accurate and relevant resources, solve challenging problems with peer assistance, conduct effective presentations employing supporting argumentation with current research, or prepare coherent essays incorporating citation and analysis.

As a result of Common Core use across the nation, there will be clear evidence for students, parents, teachers, colleges, and employers that students can demonstrate their learning. It will provide more documentation of students' competence than just achievement of "basic proficiency" scores on a test. However, the ability to develop an effective, standardized method to assess student learning for state and national purposes continues to be difficult.

Implementing these Common Core standards presents real challenges. For many students, just doing the work may not be enough. They will need to show they "know" knowledge and can employ it. For teachers and administrators who have relied on textbooks, lectures, and quiet time to guide their teaching for the last ten-plus years, they will have to relearn how to plan, employ resources, interact with students and parents, and measure real student learning.

Parents as well need to be aware that, as education changes, there will be uncertainty about how to help students with homework such as writing persuasive essays, citing several competing sources, and integrating/analyzing an author's point of view. Or they may need to let children figure out on their own how to employ algebraic and geometric thinking from class lessons to solve challenging, real-world problems.

In the end—meaning the end result of schooling—students should to be able to live and act as responsible citizens, in all that entails, and not just be able to define the word "citizen." Students should be able think on their own, work with others, and solve complex problems using a variety of resources. I think that is a goal we can all strive for.

ESSAY 8:

TEACHING: THE ROLE
OF A LIFETIME

When I first entered the teaching profession, it was not because of some grandiose dream about having an impact on society as a whole or making a difference in the goals and aspirations of a younger generation. It came down to the fact that I enjoyed being around teenagers and their energy. I also seemed to have an affinity for the social sciences, and I needed a job with benefits. After working for a few years, I recognized that I could serve as an example of what an effective adult, whether parent, businessman, professional athlete, or entertainer, might be. A role model. Being an effective role model for young people is what all teachers should aim for and is what most teachers become.

Charles Barkley, a former NBA basketball player and current television analyst, is renowned for his bold and sometimes controversial public statements. On one occasion, he stated that athletes should not be considered role models. He indicated that just because he was a beast on the court and could dunk a basketball, that didn't mean he should be viewed as a role model for kids. That role should be filled by their parents.

In response, Karl Malone, another former NBA player and a member of the Hall of Fame, stated that being a role model was not a decision an individual could make. People do not choose to be role models; they are chosen. The decision is simply whether to be a good one or a bad one.

We often hear news about the teachers who engage in inappropriate behaviors—having physical or sexual relationships with students, for example—because these examples attract the greatest publicity. However, there are more than 3.5 million teachers in the United States who act with the greatest propriety and serve their students with great care, about whom we never hear a thing. Absolutely, the rotten apples should be removed from public consumption, but you don't throw away the entire orchard when you find one.

As teachers, we are often called upon to be the chosen ones. Whether the students in our classes are from parents of wealthy or poor families, educated or illiterate ones, foreign-language or native speakers, we teachers, because of our position, have a unique opportunity, and even a responsibility, to emulate the characteristics of caring leadership.

Characteristics of our role may be simple outwardly observed behaviors such as appearance, punctuality, positive attitude, or even our use of manners. Personally, I always wore a pair of casual slacks, a collared shirt, and dress shoes, except on Fridays, when I might wear jeans and a school logo shirt. That was me and not how I expect everyone should appear. I greeted students at the door with a handshake or maybe a high five or fist pump, saying, "Good morning," "Welcome to class," or "Glad you could make it." I spoke to them with courteous language such as, "please," "thank you," "excuse me," and "ladies and gentlemen." And I always excused them with, "Have a nice day." I even made a concerted effort to know the names of all of my one hundred fifty-plus students at the end of the first week of school.

If teachers' work is done correctly, a proper relationship is established between youths and figures of authority. A teacher is not a parent, nor a friend. A teacher is not there to be liked, although hopefully the relationship develops into a positive one. A teacher's role is one of providing respect for the student and not judgment of his or her appearance, prior behaviors, race, ethnicity, or native language. Also, a teacher sets an example by demanding a student display proper respect in return, both to the teacher and to other students in the class.

In addition, a major role that teachers play is to establish classroom norms as well as behavior and performance expectations. Students from all backgrounds require the consistency of such expressions. During class, the teacher demonstrates being a role model by accepting student comments and questions, then reciprocating with respectful responses.

Outside of school, the teacher continues to fill that role, whether by choice or happenstance. When attending a student extracurricular event, a civic function, or just shopping for groceries, to the student, the teacher is still the teacher.

Furthermore, once the effective relationship is established, students often look to the teacher as a counselor, advisor, confidant, and supporter. Teachers, as role models, develop the ability to discern the health and well-being of their students, not only in terms of content learning, but in their overall general welfare. Unfortunately, there are always a few who damage the profession's reputation.

Acting as role models allows teachers a year-long period of time to influence students, not to counteract parental choice, but to offer a place of open communication. At times, a teacher may need to play the heavy, insisting on a certain level of decorum. On other occasions, he or she may offer a sympathetic ear for student concerns. During class discussions, teachers can provide a safe space for the exchange of ideas and opinions. They can share appropriate stories of their own experiences regarding educational attainment, economic challenges they have faced, or activities related to the course content in which they have participated, such as science experiments or historical engagement.

In addition, teachers can and should be role models for life skills, such as being readers, exercising, and exhibiting proper eating habits. We may be the only individuals in the students' lives who perform those functions.

We all recall our own teachers. Some we remember as being spectacular, and a few may have been horrific. The vast majority, though, performed their jobs to the best of their abilities and behaved professionally. In most instances, the influence that teachers had on students' lives did not manifest immediately. Only through the accumulation of the actions of dozens of caring, thoughtful professionals were we led in new directions.

Having the opportunity to serve as a role model for students was one of the most rewarding experiences of my career and one that most teachers, myself included, cherish.

ESSAY 9:

GOOD TEACHERS MUST BE KEPT

Teachers need job protection. Not those teachers who are abusive or grossly incompetent or lazy. Not first-year teachers or probationary ones.

However, for the rest of the teaching profession, tenure is not only a good idea, but also a necessary one to preserve the integrity and independence of the profession. It is also in the best interest of students, teachers, and the community at large.

The purpose of teacher tenure is to offer a degree of job security for high-quality teachers against administrators who may discriminate against certain teachers for personal, non-educational reasons, such as teachers' having expressed disapproval over school policies or acting to protect student interests against administrations. But it is really much more valuable than that. Teachers need to be protected against politically influential parents and swings in public sentiment on social issues.

The vast majority of teachers perform an invaluable and tremendously admirable job in the face of significant political, economic, and social challenges. Those who can, teach. They do a job most people cannot or will not do, and they do so because they care about students and their learning.

Teachers are working each day to teach not only the subject-matter content, but also life skills, values, and discipline. Even more importantly, teachers are helping students learn how to think.

That objective requires getting students to doubt, to question, to consider alternatives and perspectives in order to grow, both as students and as people. Achieving this requires risk on the part of the student and, especially, the teacher who promotes that growth. And that raises the potential for controversy, which generates new doubts and questions.

That is the reason for tenure.

In a high school English class, for instance, students might be assigned to read novels such as *To Kill a Mockingbird*, which deals with race; *The Scarlet Letter*, which addresses the subject of adultery; or *Fahrenheit 451*, which examines censorship.

Controversy.

In a social studies class, topics including revolution, immigration, or the Bill of Rights might have to be examined through primary source material. This might generate discussions of various political and economic theories, human rights, or our individual liberties (e.g. freedom of religion, press, or assembly).

Controversy.

In a biology course, students will, of necessity, be exposed to issues such as evolution and the origin of species, physical anatomy, and human sexual functions.

Controversy.

In the recent court case Vergara v. California, a judge ruled that tenure laws in California were discriminatory because tenure and seniority allowed grossly incompetent teachers to remain at the poorest schools, denying students an equal opportunity education. Those aspects of the system need to be changed.

However, in order to remove a teacher who is deemed unqualified from a classroom, an effective determination of his or her practice must be monitored and documented. That requires regular visits to classrooms and ongoing communication between teacher and evaluator. Also, remediation and professional development must be made available to offer options for growth. These observation and evaluation measures are unevenly practiced today.

Should that determination be based upon students' test scores? Maybe they should be included as one ingredient of evaluation, but not the entire basis of it. There are too many mitigating factors. Students may be academically advanced or need remediation, and significant numbers of students may be second-language learners. Teachers themselves may be assigned to new course subjects or grade levels, and it takes time to adjust— teaching remedial pre-Algebra to ninth graders is vastly different from teaching calculus to twelfth graders, and going from teaching ninth-grade world geography to twelfth-grade economics is also a big change.

All teachers are familiar with and frustrated by unqualified, incompetent, and lazy peers at their schools. They know that the performance of those teachers reflects negatively on them as professionals, and they reject the comparisons to them or the profession at large.

Based on America's ever-changing demographics, the reduced role parents play in general, and the rapidly changing climate of competition in higher education and employment, surely adjustments should be made to present tenure laws.

There should be changes in the time it takes for a person to earn tenure, as well as an increase in the amount of support services made available to help teachers improve, enhancement in the qualifications and training for evaluators who mentor struggling teachers, and reduction in the cost/process for removal of those documented as incompetent.

Even though issues relating to permanent lifetime tenure do indeed need to change, teachers also need protection from personal repercussions, unqualified administrators, and political correctness. Creating a thought-provoking curriculum is still essential to the wellbeing of our next generation of citizens. That is critical for all of us.

By protecting teachers' ability to teach, we can enhance our students' ability to learn.

ESSAY 10:

ACTUAL LEARNING KEY TO MAKING THE GRADE

Okay, let us see if this Socratic-style questioning strategy helps to broach the issue of grading in schools:

What is the purpose of education? What constitutes real learning? Are learning, knowing, and understanding all the same thing? What is the difference between knowing something and doing something? Is there a difference between learning for college and learning for employment? How is learning measured?

And finally, how does a grade in class reflect the answers to any of the above questions in a way that represents a value to the student, teachers, school, parents, colleges, or employers? Education has to mean something, so what is it?

Grading in schools has been a constant for as long as schools have been a functioning part of modern, post-industrial society. Whether the grading is used to determine success in a specific course, as a factor in calculating the receipt of a high school diploma and graduation, as part of the GPA (grade point average) calculation for college admission, or as part of a transcript/resume an employer wants to review for hiring purposes, grades are also supposed to signify that something has been learned. But what, exactly?

How grades are determined is a very complex issue that should be re-envisioned if they are going to carry meaning for our future.

In schools, particularly high schools, a variety of mechanisms are often employed in classes to evaluate students' progress and make a determination of the final grades to be awarded. This range of categories might include, but is not limited to, attendance, homework completion, pop quizzes, projects, notebooks, participation, essays, objective tests, extra credit, etc.

Sounds reasonable, right? Well, look closer and questions arise as to the value of these tasks in determining real learning or understanding.

One student may attend every class, engage readily in all class activities, complete all assignments on time, prepare highly organized notebooks, score moderately well on small quizzes, and search out and submit all extra-credit points available. In terms of points earned, this student is near the top of the class. However, on the final assessment of knowledge, whether by essay test, objective response activity, research paper, or oral presentation, the student fails, or nearly does so. Should that student receive a grade of A- or B+ if the points calculate that grade, even though learning has not been demonstrated?

A second student might be termed your classic underachiever. The student is often late or misses classes here and there, often unexcused. He or she behaves lethargically in cooperative class activities, misses assignments or submits them late, and never bothers to complete extra-credit offerings. This student is scoring near the bottom of the class register. However, when large-scale assessments including unit, quarter, and final exams are given, the student excels. Core knowledge is demonstrated and integrated understanding is comprehensive. Should this student still receive a D? After all, didn't this student learn and understand the material?

Schools today are tasked with an unbelievably extensive array of requirements to fulfill in order to promote student learning. On one hand, there is the content component. There is a core base of subject-matter knowledge that students are expected to acquire. A larger issue, however, is the teaching of the skills and processes necessary to apply that knowledge.

In terms of grading, however, schools need to focus on the knowledge and its application. That requires a real shift in what is counted toward a grade. Components such as attendance, homework, participation, notebooks, or extra credit (whatever that entails) should not be part of the actual grade.

While these aspects of education need to be taught and fostered, and the students rewarded or punished accordingly, these items do not constitute actual learning in terms of content or application. They may be part of formative assessment, meaning that they are steps toward the end goal, but they should not be counted in summative assessment to determine whether the student understands the material or its application.

The clearest example might be in mathematics, but it can be applied to all subjects. A student turns in all the homework and extra credit all year and even attends tutoring, but in the end cannot successfully calculate and process the problem correctly. Should that student pass?

Too many times, students, parents, and teachers get "doing the work" confused with actually understanding the material. If we want education to be meaningful and the grade to count for something that benefits everyone, then the methods we use for accurately measuring learning must make the grade.

ESSAY 11:

DEEPER LEARNING
THROUGH PROJECTS

Create a children's book that includes ten significant highlights, organized chronologically, which trace the development of the Civil Rights Movement from 1865 to 1965. Work with a partner. Include on each page a description of the event in your own words, as well as specific dates, vocabulary, personalities, etc., to demonstrate your understanding of the selected feature. In addition, include a visual to accompany each event. Make sure to compose your script in the language of a fourth- or fifth-grade student.

When you have finished, be prepared to visit a local elementary school to read and discuss your book with the students.

As an assessment, you will select two to four separate events that you describe in your book. Using those events, develop a compare-and-contrast essay analyzing the impacts of those events upon the political, economic, or social fabric of the United States.

The purpose of projects such as these in schools is to help make learning authentic. Simply learning names, dates, formulas, and conjugations does not instill an understanding of the material and provide value to the learner.

Projects reinforce and help students to internalize the material covered in class, and they require students to engage in life skills utilizing research, reading, writing, organization, and presentation. Projects also require students to assume both individual and group responsibility.

An additional benefit of projects is that they allow students the opportunity to engage in real learning, as they would on the job and in society. They also allow teachers opportunities to match different learning styles with a variety of tasks that connect with students' abilities. Projects can facilitate student choice, much like life, while providing teachers with a method to individualize instruction.

Several prominent educational theorists, including Art Costa (*Habits of Mind*), Robert Marzano (*Dimensions of Learning*), and Grant Wiggins and Jay McTighe (*Understanding by Design*), have detailed the value of processing learning in a meaningful way to promote a deeper and more applicable manipulation of knowledge.

An actual project assigned students in a twelfth-grade economics course required students to go out into the community to apply course knowledge and life skills.

During introductory units in economics, vocabulary such as *opportunity costs, diminishing marginal utility, elasticity of demand,* or *factors of production* can seem vague, intimidating, and lacking in significance.

Therefore, students were assigned to go out into the community in groups of three, with each group conducting an interview with a small business owner or manager to see how the concepts apply to the real world.

Each group was required to contact the individual a week ahead of time, make an interview appointment, compose questions in advance, conduct a thirty-minute interview, take notes, and send a thank-you card.

With that information, each individual student was instructed to write his or her own three- to five-page paper discussing how the individuals and businesses that were the subjects of their interviews applied the course concepts to their specific operations.

At that point, each group of three was instructed to plan a ten-minute infomercial-style class presentation, for which they were required to employ two forms of current technology (DVD, PowerPoint, audio recording) as well as skits, graphs, or posters, etc., using humor, class engagement, and class terminology, all to demonstrate understanding of how economics apply in our commercial society. These tasks allowed each student an opportunity to connect the real world of the business to the theoretical world of economic terminology and promoted a deeper understanding of the information.

In many ways, projects tie together the disconnected threads of knowledge in course content. Imagine having various ingredients such as lettuce, tomatoes, carrots, beans, and avocados laid out on a table. It looks good, but to make it a salad, you need to combine them into a bowl. Project-based learning is the "salad" that makes all the separate course concepts make sense.

Projects do not have to be quarter- or semester-long affairs in order to have value. In many instances, they can be simple tasks such as interviewing people from the present or the past to connect students to their communities. Projects can utilize students' connections to the school or community with their current units of study to provide a bridge to prior knowledge.

Students could interview people who lived through the Great Depression or the Vietnam War and then consolidate and present information. They might also research the impacts of certain scientific innovations or the circumstances around which a novel was set. Students could communicate with former immigrants or refugees to hear first-person stories; they might discuss economic savings, investment, or retirement plans with their parents to help them analyze their parents' personal decision-making processes.

Projects are more than just creating posters or dioramas. They should, in many ways, mimic what adults do each and every day, whether in college or at work. They should require students to take responsibility, gather information, interpret that information, and communicate their understanding of the information.

If we want students to function in the real world, schools need to train them to do so. Projects are major instruments that facilitate that connection, for both students and the community at large.

ESSAY 12:

GRAY AREAS: TEACHING POLITICS IN AN ELECTION YEAR

"The most difficult subjects can be explained to the most slow-witted man if he has not formed any idea of them already; but the simplest thing cannot be made clear to the most intelligent man if he is firmly persuaded that he knows already, without a shadow of a doubt, what is laid before him."

~Leo Tolstoy, *The Kingdom of God is Within You*

Tolstoy's words perfectly encapsulate the challenge high school teachers of government face when they attempt to explain the history and operations of the United States political system in a presidential year. On the one hand, when teaching the structure of the caucus and primary system, delegates, conventions, and Electoral College, for example, most students are often unaware of the facts and focus attentively to try to comprehend these concepts.

However, once the discussion turns to issues and candidates, then all hell breaks loose because they generally come to class with fixed preconceived notions obtained from their parents, friends, church, or the media, which have convinced them of the righteousness of their views.

Hence, the "gray areas" allusion. The challenge for teachers is in assisting students in opening up their minds in order to critically examine evidence-based information, and in using that information to discuss their ideas in a civil democratic dialogue with their peers. The intent of this education is to train students to employ the use of reason and civility rather than dictatorial, ideological, religion-based, gender-based, party, or race-based prejudice.

While it may be accurate to recall Barry Goldwater's quote from the 1964 presidential campaign, "Extremism in the defense of liberty is no vice," remember that Goldwater was severely trounced in the election.

The challenge still exists in defining what constitutes extremism and also in interpreting the meaning of liberty. One person's view of liberty may be another's extremism.

Increasingly in our society and political system today, extremism is an accepted position on issues, candidates, and national politics. We often fail to realize that the objective of the Constitution is to serve the people of the whole country, not a particular person, group, or ideology. It was designed that way. Factionalism, where one group dominates another, was one of the framers' biggest fears, and they worked hard to prevent it.

The framers, including James Madison and Alexander Hamilton, were very worried about and fearful of mob rule, or "mobocracy," the term they used for popular or direct democracy, which they feared would leave too much power in the hands of the people. They also were afraid of tyranny, which is why they put so many restrictions on the executive branch. They wanted a representative democracy, to both slow the shifting emotions of the people and limit the power of the president. Their intention was to purposefully slow down legislation. A certain degree of gridlock was their objective.

The framers also worked to divide powers between the national government and the states, called federalism—again, trying to protect their understanding of liberty for society. They tried to devise a system that limited the rule of the minority faction or extremist group, whether it be a racial minority, a religious minority, or a particular lobby, such as the gun lobby or the environmental lobby.

Those are some reasons why, in today's political system, so little actually gets accomplished. There must be a degree of consensus or compromise in order to create laws or take them away. The only thing that does seem to get accomplished is the creation of more bureaucracy, as more rules and procedures are enacted to address the myriad of regulations created by representatives on both sides of the political aisle.

Thus, when a real initiative from the president, Congress, or the courts does become enacted, the people or groups opposed to that action become outraged and take action. They feel that their side lost and, as a result, move to a more extreme position rather than toward the middle.

In some ways, and I know this seems very simplistic, but in terms of teaching high school students, it is particularly challenging. Yet, it also provides a great opportunity to assist them in understanding these concepts.

On most topics, the vast majority of people in this country fall into the moderate range. Yet there are those individuals or regions of the country that are strongly conservative on almost all issues, but that is their right. Conversely, there are those people who are largely liberal, and that, too, is their right. Being labeled a liberal or conservative, radical or reactionary, does a disservice to the advancement of dialogue.

Students should be taught the value of tolerance and compromise. On issues ranging from immigration to climate change, gun control, welfare, race relations, or national security, there is no one right perspective. There is a vast amount of gray area where slices of opinion vary. Students must recognize that the examination of those gray areas is where their growth as learners happens. Learning how to employ scientifically based research, evidence, and reason to examine not only their beliefs and values, but the perspectives of other students as well, is the objective of teaching an effective course of United States government.

A teacher's job is to help foster that need and indoctrinate students into the world of thinking, not just to adhere to a defined dictated ideology.

Students also should be taught that each person's ideas have a right to be heard, discussed, debated, even forcefully argued and defended. But defended by the force of words, not physical force. Just because a student holds a perspective contrary to another's does not make that person wrong. Also, just because a student and his family, friends, church, club, gender, race, TV channel, or radio station holds a contrary view does not make that view correct. Teachers need to facilitate these interactions to allow all voices to be heard and even play devil's advocate by raising contrary views when they are not presented by the students. Teachers must convey the importance of freedom of speech, religion, press, assembly, and petition, not specifically which way to practice those rights.

To quote F. Scott Fitzgerald, "The test of a first-rate intellect is the ability to hold two opposing ideas in mind at the same time and still retain the ability to function." I would suggest that students might benefit from more than just two opposing views.

Secondly, teaching about individual candidates running for office is an area particularly rife with conflict in classrooms. A candidate should not be referred to as evil or idiotic, but as having areas of strength or weakness based on a person's point of view. The opposition candidate is not "that damned liberal" or that "right-wing nut job." Neither should the elected candidate be called "the worst president ever" or "the savior of our country." That again is the extremist view of, "We won, you lost, too bad."

Teachers need to foster questioning with regard to students' beliefs, to move them off the ideological anchors that they cling to. The same thing can also be said of the public in general.

During the section of my government course in which students studied political ideology and elections, they would often inquire about my own affiliations. I never told them, but I did offer explanations as to why I could be considered to have allegiances to one or the other party. At the conclusion of the term, they were allowed to try and identify my party affiliation and/or the candidate for whom I likely voted. Invariably, about half of the students in the class selected one political leaning and half the opposite. I never did tell them. That was not my objective.

Students should be taught that there are a multitude of viewpoints that have been influenced by many sources. In addition, it should be made clear that those views don't have to be black and white; there are many gray areas, and they make the difference.

Teaching government and politics in an election year is an exciting endeavor. Almost all of the material that is presented in the course work is correspondingly taking place each day in the media. This presents a wonderful opportunity for students to see how their learning applies. The challenge is to open up the gray matter of their brains to the gray areas of issues and candidates.

ESSAY 13:

ADDRESSING ILLITERACY

The myriad challenges to be addressed in confronting and correcting the issues of illiteracy in our community are overwhelming and, in some ways, beyond comprehension.

If you can read and understand the above statement, then you are among a dwindling number of our citizens who are fortunate enough to be capable of accessing, digesting, processing, and expressing written information.

The benefits of a literate population include greater opportunities for employment and income and a reduction of poverty. It means a better life for children and a community that desires restrictions on drugs, gangs, and crime so that those children can grow up healthy and educated.

Literacy also contributes to an expanding body of consumers and therefore to an expanding collection of companies willing to provide goods and services to those consumers.

Also, a literate population means a society that is engaged in the understanding of, and communication with, various other segments of the community. It means working together to promote the well-being of the community at large. It means a population that is engaged in civic participation and democracy.

Most research has shown that children who are not reading at grade level by the end of third grade are at the greatest risk of dropping out of high school. Schools cannot do this alone. It does take a village to raise a child—a literate one.

In many of today's schools, vast numbers of students are from broken families, are significantly poor, or speak languages other than English. Often, students enter school unable to recite the alphabet, recognize letters or sounds, or add two and two. Many homes do not have reading materials or computer access, nor the skills needed to utilize them.

Schools and teachers are doing more effective teaching today than at any time in our history, employing a much greater variety of skills and strategies to assist students in acquiring literacy and numeracy to succeed. However, the demands are also greater than ever before.

Today, schools, teachers, students, and the greater society need your help to address illiteracy.

In many instances, cities and community organizations do attempt to provide literacy activities for their citizens. These obviously include public libraries but also literacy day programs or newspaper sections dedicated to literacy topics.

However, just offering options is not enough. In too many cases, these programs are applicable to people who don't have funds to participate or access to the information. They cannot attend the events or subscribe to publications.

Instead, people and programs should be bringing literacy to them. An example of this is an organization like Rotary International, in which members of the community go to schools to deliver dictionaries or read books to students.

However, even those are just one-day events of only twenty or thirty minutes each. It's a nice feel-good activity for the presenters, but there's not a great benefit to the students. What we need is a greater degree of dedication and involvement from members of the community.

One significantly helpful activity is to volunteer in schools to work with students, especially those in grades K-3. Find a school, preferably one that is low performing, and ask to help. First, you must pass a background check, but then you can commit as much time as you are able to helping with reading activities or assisting with math tutoring.

Or if time is a concern for you, perhaps you can look for an organization that already works with schools and donate funds toward purchasing books. North Stockton Rotary Club has a program in which members purchase CD players and books with accompanying CDs for several schools. Students in kindergarten and first grade can check out the materials, like at a library, and take them home to read with parents or siblings, then exchange them for others.

Public libraries should employ roaming buses that travel to the poorest neighborhoods to provide mini-classroom scenarios. They could dedicate a section of each bus that would operate like a preschool reading room and another section to help parents with English, reading, or computer lessons. Local university education programs, businesses, or community organizations might contribute people or resources to assist in this endeavor.

In order to create a society that benefits all of us, we all need to be on the same page. The key to accessing that page—and the entire book—is literacy. The future of our society lies not with the rich man, nor with the individual sage, but with an entire citizenry that is competent, capable, and caring.

ESSAY 14:

THE SEASON OF HOPEFULNESS

In many religions, cultures, and communities, the month of December and the turning of the new calendar page hold special significance. It is a time of belief, a time of giving, and a time of hope. This season is supposed to promote reflection on the events of the year past and excitement about the potential of the upcoming year. These seasonal experiences are especially true for children as they anticipate this joyous time of year.

The act of believing anchors us. It anchors us to a hope that our lives and our world can be better. We all need to believe in something, and I believe in the potential of America's youth.

Without America's youth, we cannot be. With them, all things are possible. They are us. We need to believe in our youths' potential if we have any hope of improving as a society.

During the thirty-four years that I spent as a high school teacher, and the last five serving as a volunteer for elementary-aged students, one thing hasn't changed: Kids are still kids.

Once inside the four walls of a classroom, given an opportunity to establish relationships and meet high expectations, young people are just as capable, and possess just as much potential, as they ever have.

They continue to have dreams and goals, to express curiosity given the right stimuli, and to display passion and imagination. In the end, students continue to desire acceptance and connection to the larger world—our world.

Young people today display attributes that will only serve to strengthen our communities, if they are employed effectively. They are a more diverse group, being exposed on a daily basis, in person and through the media, to a greater variety of economic, political, religious, and cultural views and images than ever before. Young people often tolerate cultural differences much more readily than earlier generations. They possess an awareness of themselves and their surroundings that can be attributed to their having had access to a wider variety of experiences than we had in the past. And in terms of technology, young people today constantly accept, adapt to, and employ it almost as a birthright. They utilize new devices and applications without a second thought.

Sure, their fashion styles and music interests have changed, and, unfortunately, so have their language and manners. Many young people resent authority and prefer to do things their own way, which may turn out to be wrong. But those things have always defined generational gaps.

Young people seem to be overly affected by peer pressure, and they also lack effective, positive role models. They often acquire their role models through mass media—music personalities or professional athletes—and not in the manner of mature judgement and responsibility.

So as a season of giving approaches, find something of value to give to a young person. Do something that improves his or her health or communication skills, reading skills or love of the outdoors. Instead of technology, give this young person a book; better yet, read it together. Instead of playing Xbox with this young person, go outside and ride bikes together. Instead of going to a fast food restaurant, take him or her to a museum. Instead of talking, listen.

Even for those of us who are not raising children anymore, we can still serve as role models for how we expect society to function. That can simply be the gift of manners. Offering up a regular "please," "thank you," or "excuse me" can set a tone. Waving another car through at an intersection or making sure to practice etiquette with a cell phone can serve as demonstrations of common good for others to follow.

Many of us have achieved success, often through education and hard work. We confronted mountains and were able to climb them. We gained experience and confidence. We learned the value of persistence. As a result, we have acquired our "gift" of hope and solidified our beliefs.

Look around at America's youth and realize that they too face challenges. The degree to which they can confront and overcome those challenges will be reflected in the shape of our future.

In many ways, young people are a reflection of the greater society. Sometimes, the pictures of the world around us can be upsetting. If we don't like that reflection, we need to change it. Children are a place to start.

Problems certainly exist, but the possibilities for solving them are even greater. Deep down, the kids are all right.

We have to believe in them and their potential if we are going to have a chance of any future at all. We can help them reach that potential.

ESSAY 15:

CREATING "EQUAL ACCESS"

Believe it or not, all students are special, all are at risk, and all need attention. Educational institutions constantly struggle to find a sense of equilibrium in providing the resources to meet the diverse needs of all students.

That means addressing the old economic problems of scarcity and opportunity costs. There are not enough resources, whether dollars, infrastructure, or personnel, to adequately meet the needs of all students. Choices must be made.

On one side of the dilemma, many students who fit the definition of "physically or cognitively handicapped" can generally be clearly identified. They might be students who are blind, deaf, or wheelchair bound. Other students might have birth defects, such as Down's syndrome, or severe intellectual disabilities that limit how they function in general educational settings.

On the other side, we have the general student population making up the majority of school populations. They have the overall skills and learning capabilities to successfully function within the school system, to graduate, and to move on to higher education or employment. However, in many ways, they too can benefit from extra attention as they attempt to maneuver the obstacles of today's complicated social norms.

In the middle, a myriad of other students exists who are not so easily identified. These students may include students on the autism spectrum, which can range from mild to severe. These might be students who have medical conditions, like Tourette's, or who have weaknesses when it comes to processing material, such as dyslexia. Also, there are students who significantly struggle with comprehension, study skills, or organization and therefore get lost in the curriculum. Any child of immigrants may speak a second language with varying degrees of fluency.

To complicate the issue, schools attempt to address the needs of students who are affected with Attention Deficit Disorder (ADD) and Attention Deficit Hyperactive Disorder (ADHD), which may be diagnosed or not, and medicated or not, but whose behaviors interfere with their learning and, often, the learning of classmates.

In addition, numbers of students possess significant emotional and behavioral issues emanating from such external factors as abuse, homelessness, extreme poverty, or just poor parenting. Or they may confront internal challenges, such as psychological conditions that require professional attention.

Now come the difficult decisions that affect the students, the schools, and society at large. How are those challenges to be addressed given the lack of resources available to achieve the learning objectives? How can schools provide "equal access" to learning?

Lincoln Unified School District in Stockton, Calif., for example, has an annual budget of approximately $71 million. Of that, about $9 million is designated for "special education" services. These obligations must be met due to federal or state government mandates regarding how these services are administered. However, the federal government appropriates only $1.3 million to fund these mandates, and the State of California contributes another $1.3 million. That only equals $2.6 million of the $9 million expense. Therefore, the remaining $6.4 million must be directed from the district's overall budget to efforts to achieve the required objectives. Other districts face similar challenges.

In turn, then, which students should be immersed in the general curriculum, and which students should be provided with a learning environment that is separate and distinct from others? And how should the available resources be allocated to maintain the appropriate education for all?

Should students with learning challenges be included in the regular classroom part of the day or the entire day? What modifications to the students' learning should be made, and by whom? Who should make these determinations?

And finally, the big issue: To what degree do the needs of one set of students (e.g. the general student population) conflict with the needs of special-education-identified students, and how can these needs best be met by teachers and schools?

Most parents desire the best educational outcomes for their children, whether that's college-level rigor or functional independence. Unfortunately, parents can be one of the major problems in confronting the issue of equal access and the legal requirement that services be "free and appropriate" to learning. There are those parents of special needs students who work to assist the schools. They act as positive intermediaries, looking for reasonable adjustments that the school can adopt and helping their children in achieving goals.

However, there are other parents who interfere with and disrupt with the process, constantly dragging in advocates and lawyers, threatening to sue, distracting teachers and school officials from serving their other students while demanding unreasonable modifications to learning.

Teachers within individual classrooms are often faced with unrealistic expectations and inadequate resources to manage all of these challenges. One set of students can create a tremendous disruption to effective learning for another. Other times, the sheer number of students will reduce the attention a teacher can and would like to provide to a learning-challenged student.

Schools and teachers face an overwhelming challenge in working to create "equal access" for students. If we truly do want the best for all members of our community, then schools must be provided with the resources to accomplish this mission.

ESSAY 16:

A MARSHALL PLAN

California ranks near the bottom among states in terms of spending per pupil. The state also ranks the highest in the nation in terms of teacher-to-student ratio, meaning it has some of the largest classes. Similar statistics apply to other states, such as Oklahoma, Arizona, or Indiana in terms of per-pupil spending or Michigan, Oregon, or Utah with regard to class size.

Also, according to the 2014 publication of the California Schools Report Card, the state scores a D for its STEM (science, technology, engineering, and math) offerings, a D in Teacher Training and Evaluation, a D in innovation and technology in schools, and a C in preschool education. Several other categories are assigned low scores as well. Surely these results are not a coincidence.

Reforms, effective reforms, must be enacted to alter the downward slide of our educational system. But which reforms? Enacted by whom?

Over the last twenty or so years, numerous reform band-aids have been applied to stop this downward slide. They range from Teach for America to charter schools, from No Child Left Behind legislation to Common Core implementation. Each proposed remedy contains a kernel of hope or a glimmer of insight. But all of these ideas are failing to stem the tide, no matter how the political, business, or religious forces choose to exaggerate their results.

There is a significant reason for these shortcomings. Schools today are expected to do too much with too little.

Below is a partial list of components that our education system provides in addition to the academic requirements: transportation, health screening, police security, psychological and counseling services, adaptive physical education, special education and resource support services, free and reduced breakfast and lunch, education for English Language Learners, varieties of computers and digital learning equipment plus training for teachers and students in utilizing those technologies, after-school programs, athletic programs, parent education and activities, and the continual upgrades of facilities.

Schools are also constantly criticized for not providing enough in numerous academic areas besides language arts and mathematics, including the arts, social sciences, civic education, physical education, and life skills.

It is not that our schools are failing. They are drowning.

In addition to the struggles faced by schools in attempting to incorporate all of the above components, there is not enough assistance in elementary schools, from lack of parenting education to a lack of in-class instructional assistants and volunteers, to a lack of mentors for students.

Teachers do not possess enough effective training and support, both in their credential programs and at their school sites. They are also severely lacking in salary and benefits. These are some significant reasons why fifty percent or more leave before five years.

School, or the concept of school, needs to be reformulated to a different paradigm. The standard industrial age system, where students of all ages and abilities attended class in one room, where the teacher was the possessor of all things of value, where "butt-in-seat" time and homework completed determined scores, should be done and gone.

Education and our concept of what constitutes school need to be reimagined and redesigned. Then, the quantity and quality of resources necessary to succeed in this endeavor should be enlisted.

In a society where it costs $50,000 per year to attend Stanford University, one of the top schools in the world, California spends over $60,000 per year to house prisoners who have a recidivism rate of 60 percent. California spends less than $10,000 per public school student with the hopes that he or she will not end up in a prison.

At the conclusion of World War II, the president and Congress, under the leadership of Secretary of State George Marshall, instituted a rescue plan to help Europe recover after the destruction of the war. The intent was to create a strong Europe that would become a bastion of free, democratic, and economically stable countries to combat the spread of Soviet Communism.

Today, California's educational system is facing a comparable threat, not from Communism, but from the burden of an unprepared citizenry.

The biggest culprit in this scenario is not the No Child Left Behind or Common Core legislation, nor the issues of teacher tenure or violence on campus. The biggest issue is the excessive weight of responsibilities with which schools are charged and the tremendous lack of resources with which to carry them out.

The legislature and the governor need to reprioritize where the resources of the state are directed. Instead of funding prison populations, welfare programs, and additional business regulations, we must evaluate what kind of future we envision. An educated population must be at the top of the list.

Back in 1917, and again in 1941, an entire country rallied behind a poster of Uncle Sam pointing his finger and saying, "I Want You for the U.S. Army." Today, a modern Uncle Sam again needs to step to the front, this time saying, "I need you to support public education."

ESSAY 17:

A CLASS OF PUBLIC DISCOURSE

Let's talk about the classroom as a forum for public discourse. Your opinion is not right. Seriously, YOUR opinion in NOT correct. And neither is that of anyone else. That does not mean your opinion is wrong, either, but just that it is your opinion—that is all. Not fact, just opinion. That opinion is supposed to be up for discussion. Too often, people vehemently spout outlandish rhetoric as fact that supports a limited understanding of or solution to an issue.

All individuals, and especially students, bring to situations preconceived notions of what is right. Those opinions are often acquired from parents, media, even peers. For instance, when students are fans of a certain team and hate another, they explain that it's because their parents and family members have always supported a certain team, so they do too.

Often, this manner of acquiring and processing information and "truths" pertains to attitudes family or friends may have inculcated into students regarding religious or political topics.

Did their pastor preach anti-gay or pro-immigration rhetoric in church? Did their parents always watch MSNBC or Fox News and demonstratively voice attitudes against "those people" or that "expletive" politician? Was every issue always presented in a "black or white," "all or nothing," or "my way or the highway" manner?

In my high school classes, including American government, United States history, and world history, I always emphasized discussion and debate in class. The social sciences are ripe for examination of a great variety of issues: political, economic, religious, and social.

Connections to historical situations always seemed to make more sense to students if I could show parallels to current events. For example, when looking at the controversies associated with abortion, the legalization of gay marriage, or the immigration of children across the Mexican border, students find those topics a more interesting way to look at the equal access and due process clauses of the Fourteenth Amendment than a dry textbook or a collection of century-old case histories.

The above problems, by the way, do not have factually CORRECT answers, only opinions.

Controversial issues are those for which there are no concrete solutions, no matter how intransigent one's position may appear.

These topics provide opportunities for students to verbalize thoughts and feelings in an open, democratically based forum while allowing them to internalize concepts of rights embedded in our historical documents. The values include rights in conflict, balancing rights, minority rule vs. majority rights, and the rule of law.

During examination of these topics, the important lesson is not to memorize the specific words of the Constitution, nor to recall the exact rulings of court cases.

These discussions can also, if handled effectively, serve to promote listening skills, respect for others' views, processing time for rational expression, and public speaking. These are the actions that will be useful throughout one's lifetime, not the recall of a case or amendment. The lessons are those of real democracy—everyday, meaningful, civil democracy. These skills are desperately needed. And given that learning is social activity, this type of talk also helps shape new ideas for consideration.

Also, it means creating and supporting arguments by carefully examining evidence, considering both sides, valuing others' perspectives, and realizing that there are multiple ways of looking at issues.

Students needs to learn how to access information. This skill can come from reading texts or literature, discerning meaning by listening to speeches, conducting research, and participating in discussions and debates.

The task of teachers is to not provide students with the right way to view issues, but to allow them the opportunity to articulate their own views. It means teaching students to think for themselves, to employ evidence, and to create arguments that enable them to think for themselves. Often, that means the teacher needs to play the devil's advocate, forcing the student to defend/support views and effectively respond to the criticism that accompanies that defense. The teacher's job is to facilitate learning, not to pontificate.

As the current state of our politics attests, solidifying positional bunkers on completely opposite sides of an issue produces no movement in either direction and no examples for our youth.

Education is supposed to assist in fostering understanding and, through that understanding, empathy for the alternate perspectives, resulting in compromise and growth as a society.

Now, of course, these views are just my opinion, not fact. They are open for discussion—a civil, democratic discourse that attempts to promote understanding.

Have an opinion? Let's talk about it.

ESSAY 18:

THE BATTLEGROUND OF
TEACHER EVALUATIONS

There are some terrible, horrible, no good, very bad teachers out there, to tweak a beloved title. There always have been and there always will be. There were poor teachers in school when I was a student and when you were young. There are poor teachers in your kids' schools today. However, the vast majority of teachers are professional, dedicated individuals who work extremely hard and perform tasks that most people in our society cannot nor will not attempt.

There is an old adage regarding educators: "Those who can, do; those who can't, teach." That is hardly the case. Those who can, teach, survive, and prepare our students for the benefit of both them and our society. And most of those teachers who can't teach (almost half of all teachers leave the profession within five years) quit. It is just too difficult.

Still, teachers need to be evaluated. There must be procedures in place to determine that progress is being made in terms of student learning. Research continually demonstrates that the classroom teacher is the most important person to provide that learning.

Also, schools, districts, business owners, and taxpayers want assurances that the students are being taught effectively and that student learning does, indeed, take place. This issue of evaluation of teachers is a political hot button in both the state and national arena that will not go away.

The characteristics of what qualifies as a "good" or "bad" teacher are not always clear. How is someone supposed to be judged, and who is to be the judge, jury, and executioner in this process? As is often said, the devil is in the details.

As it typically stands now, an administrator enters a classroom once or twice a year (maybe even every other year), takes notes, fills out a checklist, and evaluates the teacher. Not very effective. However, administrators, too, have extremely hectic schedules and, even though it is probably the most valuable function that person has, there is little time. Also, some administrators are not very good at that aspect of the position, even though they may handle organization, security, budgeting, and parent communication very well.

The job description of an effective teacher is detailed with written standards regarding class management, lesson planning, assessment, student engagement, etc. Today, though, it is all about the scores. The score a student receives on a standardized test once a year seems to be measuring stick with which reformers identify "good" or "bad" teachers.

Just as in the game of baseball, where a player's home run totals are not the sole criteria of value (hits, batting average, steals, fielding, etc.), a teacher's value should not be determined solely by the results of his or her students' scores.

Care should be taken not to carve all teachers with too sharp a scalpel regarding that single score. That does a tremendous disservice to the innumerable functions teachers perform in educating our children.

There is a concept in economics called *ceteris paribus*. This Latin phrase means, roughly, "all things being equal." In schools today, all things are never equal. The number of students per day or per year constantly changes. The number of English-language learners or special-education students or students living in poverty and getting free or reduced lunch, the number of subjects being taught, the amount of involvement from parents, the revolving door of new administrators, the materials such as textbooks, the technology applied, and the expected standards or methods to be evaluated all are subject to change. It makes it very difficult for teachers to hit a constantly changing target.

Using a single score as the criteria takes some of the judgment out. It also reduces the time and effort an administrator needs to make a decision. Just check the score. But that does not improve the evaluation nor the teacher quality.

All of this being said, progress still ought to be made in more effectively monitoring teacher quality. Those very poor teachers need to be identified and then retrained or removed. The demands of today's colleges and workplaces, the fluctuations of individual students' levels of preparedness, and the expectations of employers and our democracy require that we have the best teachers available.

To achieve these challenging objectives, numerous methods of support should be developed and actuated. Evaluations should employ multiple components, and a measure of students' academic growth should be one of those. Administrators should develop systems that enable them, or someone who specializes in that area, to get into classrooms on a regular basis, to more regularly observe classroom activities and build trust with teachers.

Teacher coaches should be more readily available to assist not only struggling teachers, but also all teachers, as they adjust to the constant fluctuations that occur in the world of education.

Also, teacher unions must be more flexible and willing to bend. They cannot continue to defend the incompetent few among them and risk damaging the reputation of the vast proportion of quality educators.

Those who can teach, do, and they usually do it well. Schools must develop the proper evaluation methods to ensure trust and growth for our students and our future.

ESSAY 19:

MYRIAD REASONS WHY
TEACHERS TEACH

Teachers, both individually and collectively, seem to be the current target du jour for society's ills—illiteracy, unemployment (especially among the lower economic classes), juvenile delinquency, and government debt. Then there are all those accusations of physical, mental, and even sexual abuse by teachers. Those damn teachers!

Well, the famous French general and emperor Napoleon once said, "The true conquests ... are those that have been wrested from ignorance." Let's see if I can provide a degree of explanation to enlighten that ignorance.

Let us start with the first major misunderstanding as to why teachers teach: money, benefits, and pensions.

An average starting teacher's salary, on the West Coast, is about $45,000 a year. Figuring an average work week of fifty hours (which actually is a low estimate) for twelve months a year, that averages out to less than eighteen dollars an hour. My daughter often earns more than twenty dollars an hour for babysitting two children. Teachers have already attended college and received four-year degrees (and, for some, graduate degrees), teaching credentials, and passing scores on state-mandated competency tests. It's typical for a teacher to have more than thirty students in a class.

In terms of health benefits, they aren't free either. Teachers may contribute upwards of a $1,000 or more each per month to have those benefits for themselves and their dependents.

Yes, it is true that districts contribute a percentage to teachers' pensions—maybe seven percent of the teacher's income. But the teachers themselves contribute eight percent, and that percentage is increasing. Further, bear in mind that teachers do not receive Social Security benefits for their work when they retire.

After taxes, union dues and pension and benefits contributions, beginning teachers live on less than $2,000 per month. That means they are receiving, after taxes, something in the neighborhood of $65 per month, per child. This is what teachers earn to educate our posterity? Ridiculous!

Another misunderstanding has to do with all the "free" time teachers receive. Heck, they only work from eight in the morning until three in the afternoon. They get their summers off, have two-week breaks over the holidays and at least another week in the spring, then four or five days around Thanksgiving. Cushy life!

Well, first, consider that they need time off because they have often been in a combat-like zone after dealing with students, their parents, overbearing administrators, and the constant challenge of a changing curriculum, new resources, and testing stress.

But more importantly, during their "time off" on weekends, holidays, and school break periods, they are preparing lessons, acquiring and printing materials (often at their own expense), correcting papers, tutoring students, contacting parents, meeting with other teachers, attending school functions and conferences, attending training and continuing education classes, and communicating with counselors, administrators, and district officials.

So, then, why the hell do people choose to teach?

They teach because they care. Seriously. They believe in our youth and that they can make a difference in helping that youth to learn—not just content and technical skills, but also how to be better human beings that help improve the world in which we all live.

Teachers enjoy the energy and vitality of youth and want to influence students' thinking and their ability to function effectively and independently in the world around them.

If you have ever listened to teachers away from school, they are constantly discussing their successes or their struggles with students or their families as they strive to help students achieve.

They care because they feel passionate about the important roles of science, mathematics, history, literature, music, physical education, etc. in the world into which students will eventually be thrust.

They teach because, likely, they themselves were inspired by teachers in their own pasts and want to contribute to our children's world in the same way their own teachers once did for theirs.

Teachers see on a daily basis the challenges that students face, often because of poor parenting, when they come to school dirty, hungry, and without their homework done, struggling with their learning in the classroom or on the school grounds. Teachers want to help.

Teachers also get intensely frustrated by a lack of support both in the classroom and from their administrators and district and state policymakers, which prohibits them from helping their students learn. They strive to make sure students reach their potential, but there are so many roadblocks. Yet, they still teach.

As Lee Iacocca, former chairman of Chrysler, once said, "In a completely rational society, the best of us would choose to be teachers and the rest of us would have to settle for something else, because passing civilization along from one generation to the next ought to be the highest honor and the highest responsibility anyone could have."

Teachers care most about those members of our society that truly matter: their students.

ESSAY 20:

CHALLENGE OF ADDRESSING STUDENT NEEDS

Just mentioning the concept of segregation sends chills up my spine. As a former United States history teacher, the vision of separate facilities for black Americans in schools, restrooms, bus stations, and neighborhoods evokes one of the darkest periods in our nation's past.

In the U.S., the word *segregation* may also refer to the separation of women into predetermined positions and occupations deemed "appropriate" for their sex; the internment of Japanese Americans in camps during World War II; or the forced relocation of Native Americans to reservations. These and other forms of segregation by race, gender, class, language, or nationality should forever remain dead and buried.

But I am recommending a different kind of segregation, a much more positive one. The segregation I am referring to is the kind that would address the extreme differences in ability and behavior that exist among students in many of today's classrooms. As a result of overcrowding, lack of resources, poor parenting, behavioral disorders, and minimal classroom assistance, too many students are not receiving the individualized attention they need in order to be successful.

Schools and teachers cannot be all things to all students all of the time.

I have observed primary school classes with more than thirty students each. This is one teacher, trying to teach children of many diverse backgrounds—often including students with special emotional, mental, or physical needs. Some may not be able to sit still and are constantly jumping around the room, disturbing the rest of the class or even crawling on the floor. Other students may not speak English or have disparate levels of fluency. Some may be two or three grade levels below their peers, and others two or three above.

In these rooms, there may be no assistance for the teacher—no parent volunteers, no classroom aides, no help whatsoever.

The same is all too often true for high school classes as well.

Yet students are expected to meet specific state standards and, now, with Common Core, specific operational standards that integrate material across different levels and disciplines. Effectively teaching this material, under the circumstances, becomes impossible.

Teachers are taught to "differentiate"—that is, provide material to each student based on his or her individual needs. In addition, if they have English Language Learners (ELL) in their classes, they must work with only those ELL students for twenty to thirty minutes each day, as required by law. This leaves the rest of their students, who may only be six or seven years old, to do seatwork on their own. Can children this young really work independently?

Or suppose that some students behave defiantly and disruptively. How is the teacher supposed to handle the emotional outbursts while still providing attention to the students who are ready to learn?

The answer may be to track students according to their ability levels. We need to develop separate classes, or at least significant periods of time each day in which small groups arranged by level each get the teacher's focused attention, whether the groups are composed of students who are not yet at grade level or those who are advanced beyond grade level. This would allow students to be appropriately challenged in reading, writing, and math.

This arrangement was once employed in schools, but it was frowned upon because it was felt that some groups were designated as low level based on their races or behaviors. Or it was felt that the teachers assigned to these groups were those with the least experience or the weakest skills.

What I am proposing for today's educational environment is an alternative that meets the needs of students and teachers in an environment in which too many students are unsupported and unprepared to learn.

In truth, having students of diverse backgrounds and levels in class together is important. Requiring students to learn from others different from themselves helps promote perspective and develop patience. Teaching students to get along with others, to be both teachers and learners, is of incredible value to those who live in a democratic society.

However, the needs of the few should not consume the time and energy of the teacher and limit other students' access to education.

The idea is to reconsider segregation, not necessarily to apply it. The best alternative would be to reduce class sizes, provide additional assistance in classrooms (especially in the early grades) to help students develop the basics, hold parents accountable for their students' attendance and behaviors, and provide teachers with more effective training and resources to succeed with the vast discrepancies of learners.

The objective is not to return to the dark ages of our past but to discover an enlightened future in which all students have equal access to opportunity.

ESSAY 21:

PLAN FOR A PRODUCTIVE SUMMER

Remember when your teacher assigned you to write an essay about your summer vacation? Well, too often these days, when you ask high school students that question, they respond with something like, "Aw, I just hung around," or "I visited friends."

Really? That's all you did?

I guess those responses are slightly better than other answers I heard when I was a teacher, such as, "I slept in," or I played video games."

This type of response was not true for all students, but they were prevalent enough to get me slightly exasperated.

So it got me thinking about how I might front load potential ideas to help students make their summer vacations more productive. I attempted to frame the discussion around students' frequent complaints that they never had enough free time during the school year, that they were always too busy to have any fun.

They claimed to have too much homework, too much time committed to sports or other activities, too much time getting to and from school, etc., but they never had enough time for sleep.

Well, now they would have enough time, I told them. They would likely have more free time than they would ever have at any other time in their lives. In college, they would probably have summer classes, jobs, or internships. Their future careers likely would not provide them with ten weeks of uncommitted time. And once they started their own families, their spouses and children would by necessity demand greater incomes, time commitments, and stress. Time would really seem to be in short supply.

Knowing this, they should approach summer break with a goal of accomplishment. They should be able to demonstrate, upon returning to school, how they improved their lives and made progress in becoming better human beings.

In that spirit, I asked the students to create lists—five to be exact. Five lists of five.

On the first, they were to identify five books they planned to read (or five possible book topics). I also told them that my own personal goal every summer was ten books. Many of my students did not have books in their homes, so that would mean going to the library (yes, they still exist), downloading them onto mobile devices, or borrowing them from other people.

Next, I asked them to list five places they would like to visit. No, I wasn't looking for Mt. Everest; I wanted them to be realistic—a museum, a concert, a national park, a historic landmark, an amusement park, or a theater performance. The objective was some sort of purposeful destination where they could explore, experience, and grow.

Third, the students were asked to compile a list of five skills they would like to learn or to improve upon. Such a list might include a sport, a talent such as drawing or playing guitar, cooking, gardening, computer applications … anything.

The fourth list would include five ideas for earning money over the summer. These might be simple things like helping parents or grandparents with extra chores, or they might include mowing lawns, babysitting, painting neighbors' houses, or finding jobs.

Lastly, the students were tasked with contemplating and recording five ways that they might work toward improving their lives or the lives of others. For themselves, this could be losing weight, eating healthier, exercising more, meeting new friends, and spending time with siblings. For assisting others, it could be charitable work, helping at church, or working on a fundraiser for an organization.

I tried to impress upon students that time isn't something you can get back once it's gone. This "free time" they had could be a tremendous opportunity to truly grow as human beings, without anyone forcing them to do it.

The students weren't expected to accomplish everything on their lists. Also, they were welcome to modify items or add new ones as the summer progressed.

The overall intent of the strategy was to assist students in developing goals, planning for success, staying active and productive, forming healthy habits, and becoming better human beings in the process.

The mother of one of my students even approached me a few weeks ago and indicated that her daughter, who was at least ten years out of high school, still set the goal each summer to read five books.

So when all of you students and parents are asked about your summer, you can now proudly share all of the wonderful things you accomplished. C'mon, time's a-wastin'!

ESSAY 22:

TEACH YOUR ... TEACHERS WELL?

There is a song from 1970 by Crosby, Stills, Nash, and Young entitled "Teach Your Children" whose lyrics include the following: "You, who are on the road must have a code that you can live by," and "feed them on your dreams ... the one you'll know by."

Those lines refer to our offspring and to future generations. But they could also be applied to teachers and how prepared they are to undertake the challenges they confront in educating today's students.

Unfortunately, the code, or training, provided to prospective teachers all too often falls far short of the dream. If teachers cannot be properly trained for their profession, then the likelihood of them achieving success in the long term, for themselves or their students, also is significantly diminished.

The biggest challenge is reckoning the philosophy of education classes, credentialing programs, and the state accreditation requirements with the actual needs of classroom experiences.

There is a tremendous gap. It is the old comparison of the ivory tower philosophers versus the teacher-in-the-trenches method of preparing to teach.

After surveying all segments of the teaching realm, I believe that there are three areas worthy of examination.

The first issue includes the preteaching aspects involving the selection of qualified candidates and the credentialing coursework. Due to the tremendous shortage of teachers in all fifty states, this is particularly important.

In terms of the selection of teachers for employment, it can be a mixed bag. When the occasion exists to attend job fairs between January and April, the opportunity to select qualified candidates is fairly high. Unfortunately, due to the shortage of teachers and the late time frame in which teaching positions become available, the teachers hired in July and August often are those least suited for the profession.

Education programs need to do a better job of vetting candidates early on for effective characteristics, particularly the ability to establish positive relationships with students, work cooperatively with other teachers, reflect and grow, or display strong passion for teaching.

Of course, there is always a need for a theoretical approach to teaching, and every other profession. However, in education, there is a tremendous discrepancy between theory and practice when it comes to the realities of today's classrooms; at the least, we must be sure candidates are capable of dealing with the diverse challenges. It takes consistent exposure to today's public (or charter) school teaching environment to develop an awareness of the many challenges a teacher has to confront on a daily basis.

The teachers that I contacted (I surveyed about twenty teachers from all areas of the profession) felt that too many credentialing courses were ineffective because they simply employed "lecture, quiz, essay-type structure" and "were generally useless" or "a waste." According to one elementary teacher, "college courses involved a lot of reading and responses ... which was very useful information, but did not help in terms of how to teach or what to teach." Most teachers agreed that the college courses "were ineffective in helping deal with the wide range of performance levels in any given classroom."

Teachers felt they gained insight when their professors "brought experience and application" into their courses. The best professors were those who "simply talked shop" and that "modeled lessons and discussed roadblocks," or those who "were real classroom teachers who were knowledgeable and were able to share real experiences."

Another concern described by the teachers is the support (or lack thereof) during their student teaching or intern assignments. A knowledgeable, demanding, and committed master teacher is critical to learning how to teach. When that component is in place, the likelihood of success is greatly enhanced. Too often, however, the individuals selected to serve as master teachers are not up to par. Whether this is the fault of the credentialing institution, the school district, or the administrator is difficult to say.

In some cases, the master teacher is an absentee supervisor, tossing the new teacher to the wolves and disappearing for weeks at a time. In other cases, the individual is such a poor role model that the teacher acquires very little in the way of effective teaching methods/strategies and, in some cases, just observes what *not* to do. Often, the university itself requires too little time for "soloing" by the new teacher—only a couple of weeks—so that, consequently, the true challenges of the profession are not encountered.

Preparing teachers for today's learning environment is like shooting at a moving target. And we keep missing.

During those initial teaching years, support and assistance are critical to establishing a foothold on the battlefield of today's classroom.

In the first two years of employment, new teachers are supposed to be provided with mentors. However, the quantity of required paperwork overloads the new teacher and minimizes the mentoring aspect. Most teachers struggle with the management of disruptive behaviors and require more direction on dealing with the demands of daily operation routines, which involve students, parents, administrators, and paperwork.

The challenges of teaching in today's schools are so overwhelming that most of the general public cannot begin to conceive of their magnitude. But teachers know. They chose this profession, just as anyone might choose to be a doctor, an engineer, or a firefighter. Their dream of success means making a difference for both themselves and those they teach. But they need to have a better "code to live by," as the song lyrics say, to achieve that dream.

ESSAY 23:

THE MYTH OF FAILING SCHOOLS

"Once upon a time" is a typical opening line used in fairy tales, so let's start there...

Once upon a time, schools and teachers were responsible for the lack of improvement in students' state-mandated test scores and graduation rates. Schools where this lack was significant were labeled as "failing."

This tale from the Land of Make-Believe is unfortunately perceived by many as fact, which ignores the real problem and unfairly assigns a disproportionate amount of blame to schools.

To demonstrate, imagine trying to apply the storyline of an established fairy tale, *The Prince and the Pauper*, to the issue of failing schools.

Originally written as a book by Mark Twain in the 1880s, and then presented in Hollywood style as a movie by Disney and others, *The Prince and The Pauper* is the story of two boys who look alike but lead vastly different lives. They decide to change places and see what it's like to live the other's life.

Let's apply that same concept to schools. Imagine that the entire staff of a very high-performing school—the principal, teachers, and clerical workers—switched places with the staff of an extremely low-performing school.

What might we expect to happen? Would the students' growth and achievement drastically improve? Would these students' attendance, attitudes, work ethic, imaginations, and creativity burst onto the scene like a rainbow of energy and color? Would we then be able to eliminate that designation of "failing school" and live happily ever after? Would magic happen? Not so fast.

The students in both of these schools are still living in the same neighborhoods as before. The same parents, grandparents, family members, or foster caregivers are still raising them. Economically, things have not changed. Poverty and employment levels are still constant. The behaviors relating to alcohol and drug use, mental illness, homelessness, food insecurity, attendance, homework completion, and parental involvement remain present.

It would still be true that these students were raised for the first five years of their lives in environments that more dramatically affected their ability to perform than the schools themselves.

The students from each of these schools have been exposed to entirely different kinds of stimuli during their preschool years and throughout their educational experiences.

No amount of "abracadabra" in altering the staff, setting, or curriculum is going to alter the glaring deficits that these children face at home.

In fact, some negative results might occur from these changes. The staff members who have just been transferred from the high-performing school to the low-performing school are likely over time to become frustrated and discouraged by the lack of attendance, parental contributions, and student progress. Over time, they are sure to be labeled as part of the "failing school" scenario, and they might even leave their jobs as a result.

Meanwhile, the staff who has moved to the high-performing school might feel like a bunch of miracle workers. Their students will show up on time, complete their homework, and receive high marks on assessments. They will have numerous in-class parent volunteers, chaperones to school functions, donations to classroom resources, and supplies. They may well feel as if a fairy godmother has sprinkled them with fairy dust and made their dreams come true. They may become energized and want to put in additional time to experiment with new practices. They will no longer be considered part of a "failing school." They will be labeled "award-winning" or "highly effective"!

Schools must constantly change, adapt, and strive to do a better job, without question. And the taxpayer resources allocated by the legislature must continue to expand to assist them in achieving this task. Our society must have an educated citizenry to maintain our government, economy, and way of life.

However, it is not always the schools or their staffs that are failing in their endeavors.

All of us must recognize that the degree of poverty and illiteracy among major segments of our population is overwhelming. The hole students find themselves in before they begin attending school is often simply too deep for the school system to help dig them out.

Without a doubt, some of the criticism is deserved. Schools and teachers should be held accountable. There are indeed areas of concern in terms of how teachers are hired and evaluated, how computer technology and resources are allocated, the high numbers of students in classes, and the variety of teaching strategies and methodologies that are applied.

However, fixing those areas still may not produce the results we would hope to see.

The biggest indicators of student success and achievement are not based on academic factors; they are familial. Poverty, lack of parental education and involvement, parent incarceration, poor school attendance, alcohol and drug use at home, homelessness, and single-parent families are among the real culprits.

If members of our society desire a "happily ever after" to this fairy tale of failing schools, they must be willing to invest in improved educational outcomes for all segments of our community.

ESSAY 24:

READING: THE LANGUAGE
OF LEARNING

One of the most important skill areas teachers should emphasize is reading. In fact, reading is the only subject worth teaching students. And it is a much greater challenge than imagined.

By reading, I do not mean just learning to read written words. I also mean teaching students comprehension in reading numbers; evaluating situations (analyzing); reading other people's body language, emotions and attitudes (interpreting); and, the biggest challenge of all, reading themselves and the choices they make (reflecting).

It is imperative that schools teach to the whole child, not just teach to the test. Students must become more prepared to function and adapt in an ever-changing environment. All too often, parents do not effectively take on the responsibility of learning to "read" as identified above and, consequently, cannot model for their children how to interpret the world around them, using the aforementioned skills.

Obviously, in terms of training students to literally read, to understand words, taking the time to read is critical. This task needs to start when children are infants. Families should take advantage of the public library, Friends of the Library organizations, available preschool or Head Start programs, or even garage sales in order to acquire books. However, often due to poverty or parental illiteracy, many homes today do not have books within their walls.

It would be wonderful if parents were reading to their children every day. That could mean reading stories, product labels in grocery or department stores, names of cars on the road, street signs, or anything else that promotes reading and then taking the time to talk with kids about what they have just read.

This kind of reading involves not just phonics (sounding out words), but practicing the fluency or rhythm of sentences. It involves reviewing vocabulary, discussing meaning, comparing topics, reviewing characters, and simply modeling reading for pleasure. Schools help to facilitate these types of reading.

But this is just one type of reading that's important to a child's development. Learning to read our surroundings is another, and schools look for ways to help with this one, too.

While out on a bike ride the other day, I observed a young mother also riding a bike and towing her young child in one of those mini-trailer vehicles. She was talking to the little girl, who was maybe a year and a half in age, saying, "Look at the trees. See the big ones and the small ones, and look at the colors and shades of green." She continued to reference animals and points of reference—in a sense, assisting her daughter in "reading" her surroundings. This is a great start to literacy and one upon which schools can build.

The same is true for numbers. Numerical illiteracy is not inherited genetically, but in some ways it can be passed on. Unfortunately, some students enter school not being able to count to ten or recognize individual digits. Students often still count on their fingers in second, third, or even fourth grade and cannot multiply six times seven, even when entering high school. Of course, many students are already proficient, but too many are not. However, through the teaching of mathematics, schools work to focus on that type of "reading" as well.

Teachers instruct, practice, review, and assess this information daily. Mathematics also includes the use of vocabulary such as ratio, percent, decimals, and equal/unequal. Much of math incorporates word problems that require the interpretation and comprehension of concepts. Reading and math processing should be part of everyday conversation at home and school. Reading is critical to arriving at solutions!

Other aspects of reading relate to life in general and to decisions individuals make when they confront daily situations. This kind of reading involves awareness, interpretation, and analysis. This might be achieved through class discussion, class meetings, current events discussions, etc. Those reading lessons require reinforcement, which schools and teachers practice every day. All too often, people of all ages make poor choices that affect their lives without considering the consequences. Schools must teach students to employ certain skills in order to address these challenges.

In schools today, significant effort is employed to manage students' behavior and assist them in making well-informed and mindful choices. All the while, teachers strive to help students understand the consequences that can accrue from poor choices. That requires reading as well.

There are incentives such as star charts, treasure box toys, or raffle tickets for good behaviors, as well as correctives such as timeouts or even weekly class meetings in which students comment on each other's misbehavior and vote on consequences for poor student choices.

Schools also attempt to teach/demonstrate appropriate behaviors on the playground and in classroom activities. Many schools host school-wide assemblies wherein students are introduced to anti-bullying initiatives, instances of respectful treatment of others, and even proper manners

Finally, schools should and do instruct students to "read" themselves. This includes teaching students to examine their own states of mind, their emotional levels, and their goals. Teachers teach students to reflect on their areas of growth and areas of potential. They teach them to develop readiness to learn and organization to accomplish that learning.

Students can become successful learners as well as better citizens, but only if they learn how to read.

ESSAY 25:

A NIGHT ON THE TOWN

Along the red carpet path you strut in your top hat and tails. On each side of the red-carpeted walkway sit the stylish Packards, Studebakers, Chevrolets, and even a few Model Ts from the 30s and 40s. In the glare of the bright lights, past the bulbs of flashing cameras, you enter the hall. Before you are gambling tables galore for blackjack, roulette, poker, and craps. All is reminiscent of a Prohibition-era speakeasy. Servers offer up food and beverages to satisfy any appetite. In the background are the sounds of the jazz band emanating from the stage, where they play wonderful swing tunes from the likes of Glenn Miller and Benny Goodman. You happily greet your compatriots, who include Babe Ruth, Franklin Roosevelt, and Billie Holiday. Your name is announced: "Ladies and gentlemen, please give a warm welcome to Mr. John D. Rockefeller." Wow, what a night!

When I was a teacher of United States history, each year I would conduct this event, which was entitled "A Night on the Town." During the unit called "Search for the American Dream,"

I asked students to each research an individual who achieved fame and recognition during the first half of the 20th century. Such well-known figures as John Dillinger, Mary Pickford, Langston Hughes, Amelia Earhart, Shirley Temple, and Jack Dempsey were up for selection. Subjects could be from the realm of politics, athletics, business, music, film, or something else. Students were each required to read a biography of the personality selected and to make copious notes and citations.

The next step in their learning process included preparing a paper of approximately five typed pages, making a presentation to the class, and then appearing, in character dress, at our evening event. Throughout the unit, I also introduced them to jazz and swing dancing, even clearing the room of desks in order to practice some moves, which they had to display during the event.

Years, even decades, later, students still remember everything about that evening.

Why? Because in addition to being educational, it was FUN!

Events and activities like this used to occur with regularity in schools. High school students might experience highly animated lectures from costumed instructors followed by multiday laboratory practicums, or prepare archaeological digs by burying artifacts that then had to be exhumed by other students and analyzed.

Elementary students participated in events such as Valley Days, during which they learned to farm, create woodwork, and make horseshoes, or mission trips, where entire educational units were built around students becoming neophytes at a California mission. They wore frocks and actually performed the manual labor of making candles and weaving baskets, while pre- and post-activities included reading primary sources and writing journals of their experiences.

Throughout the school year, before high-stakes testing, opportunities existed for museum field trips to the Academy of Sciences or the de Young Art Museum in San Francisco, or guided nature outings to Indian Grinding Rock State Park. Students might also participate in the creation of school gardens, planting and cultivating vegetables and herbs while applying language arts, science, or math principles. All of these activities were vital components in bringing school and the joy of learning to life.

In other words, FUN!

Yes, students should be required to learn the basics of content, but the drill-and-kill method of memorized drudgery has its limits, and they have been reached. There is only so much of the textbook-and-worksheet style of classroom monotony that can be force-fed to students before they turn off to learning.

School is much more than textbooks, lectures, and homework. It is much more than letters and numbers. Bringing those distinct facts and details to life is what generates the imagination, curiosity, and investigation to learn more. Students need to participate in and experience the richness that learning has to offer. They need to be able to manipulate and process learning in a way that makes it real and connects to something outside the four walls of the classroom.

Too many students, due to the family poverty and illiteracy, lack exposure to the richness of learning. Many have never even seen the snow or the ocean, been to a museum or an art gallery. One former teacher remembers accompanying students to a local zoo and noticing how many of the students on the bus stared in awe at the open farmlands north of the city, because seeing them was a new experience. Others were thrilled to be able to explain how they spent their weekend taking a long trip to visit their aunt ("in Lathrop!").

The shared-experience part of community is often lost when we actually have little in common. Providing an enriching activity in which to engage students can help provide that shared experience that serves as a building block for learning.

In the last decade or two, much of the enrichment of former school days has disappeared. As a result of testing requirements, mandated curricula, and pacing timelines, field trips have been reduced or eliminated, professional development opportunities have dried up, and science and social science have often been relegated to minor subjects. Due to legitimate budgetary issues and the political climate of nuts-and-bolts learning structure dictated from on high, there seems to have been something lost in the process.

School still needs to contain an element of excitement and, even, a little bit of FUN!

ESSAY 26:

FOR WHOM THE BELL TOLLS

Well, it is that time of year again: back to school. The big yellow buses will begin circling neighborhoods, picking up students who are still sleepy but carrying new backpacks and wearing new clothes.

The students themselves are generally eager to meet their teachers and renew their friendships with classmates from last year. There also is, on their part, a little bit of trepidation. It has been more than two months since they were last in school. What has changed? Where are their classrooms? Will their teachers be nice? Who are the new cool kids?

I remember being on the high school campus and helping students and their parents follow a campus map in order to discern the best routes for getting to class on time.

But the students are also believers. They believe that this new school year will provide new learning, new activities, new friends.

Parents, too, are confronted by the new back-to-school regimen. They have to make sure that alarms are set, breakfasts prepared, children dressed and, hopefully, at school on time. This return to routine can bring some benefits. Parents no longer need day care and schools can take over the engagement and discipline of their children.

Stores, too, welcome this transition to school. The number of advertisements, from posters to mailers, catalogs, Internet ads, and radio and television commercials, inundates our senses as the back-to-school drama plays out, competing for customers' cash.

But there's another level of major excitement-versus-anxiety scenario that plays out in classrooms all over the country.

This drama holds significant challenges for teachers as well, many of which go unnoticed or unappreciated.

Teachers do not just show up on the first day of school and greet students with, "Hello, I am Mrs. So-and-So." At the conclusion of the previous school year, they often had to box up their belongings, remove items from walls, identify needed repairs, and turn in keys.

However, over that summer break, many changes may have occurred. There may have been a new curriculum developed and new textbooks and materials adopted, which they have had to read and internalize before school starts. Teachers may have to adjust to new classrooms, new subjects, or new grade levels. Teachers end up spending unpaid time to attend professional development conferences and seminars in order to learn the updated teaching frameworks and technology, and then they have to create units and lessons to incorporate these into their plans. It definitely adds to the anxiety of the upcoming year.

Then they have to prepare their new rooms and make copies of inordinate amounts of materials to distribute to students, parents, and administrators. Frequently, schools turn off their air conditioning over the summer, which limits the comfort level on those hot summer days.

In preparing to welcome the students, before that first bell tolls, teachers feel anguish over acquiring their class lists and trying to pronounce their students' names (at the high school level, that may be 175 names) so they can greet them properly. In addition, they need to refresh themselves on the rules and procedures of classroom management to effectively corral all these students, who may have had little if any structure or discipline over their break.

Teachers, too, can become a little squeamish as that first day approaches. They struggle with sleep as thoughts of students, lessons, and discipline disturb their slumber. They get nervous as the day approaches, wondering if they will be ready, getting clothes prepared and lunches made, and establishing new routines as they mentally prepare for the stresses they will face. Teachers have to get in physical shape as well as mental and emotional shape in preparation for days filled with students and schedules. Even standing, sitting, and bending all day requires some conditioning, and it may take a week or two to adjust.

However, teachers are excited about welcoming their new charges, trying to make good first impressions. They look forward to working to improve the knowledge, skills, and character of our next generation of citizens.

Veteran teachers, even those with decades of teaching experience, face these types of challenges. There is still a high degree of energy and hesitation as they engage in that eternal balance between the problems and benefits of change, for them and their charges. New teachers confront an additional set of challenges. But with a love of students and a firm hand, they too will survive.

Teachers entered this profession in order to make a difference in the lives of young people. They want to inspire students to think, to be prepared to enter the realm of adulthood. They know that it is not only for the students that the first bell sounds. Teachers, it also sounds for thee.

ESSAY 27:

A.P. CLASSES: ARE THEY
WORTH THE COST?

At what age do you think were you ready, in terms of both ability and maturity, to be enrolled in and successfully complete a college course? Fourteen? Seventeen? Twenty-one? In my case, probably never.

In high schools and classrooms across the United States, students are regularly allowed, cajoled, or even just enrolled automatically into Advanced Placement (AP), International Baccalaureate (IB), or honors courses in areas such as chemistry, literature, calculus, history, etc. These courses are supposed to be equal in content and rigor to college freshman-level standards. In many instances, students are not just taking one course of that perceived caliber, but sometimes multiple such classes each year of high school, beginning as freshmen. Some schools, often called university high schools, offer entire curricula that, on paper, qualify under this designation.

113

I believe, as Shakespeare once wrote, "something is rotten in Denmark."

First, some background. Decades ago, there were no Advanced Placement-type courses available for students. Students might be "tracked" into different levels of courses, such as honors, general education, or remedial. Often, these labels might indicate to administrators who was ready for college, who might be, and who likely would not be. However, there was no high-stakes testing attached to these courses. Unfortunately, students were often channeled into these courses through a variety of factors including race, gender, language, learning difficulties, attitude, etc.

As these labels have gone out of vogue in the last twenty-five to forty years, Advanced Placement courses have taken their place. Originally, they were offered in just a few areas, usually English, history, science, or math. Students were incentivized to enroll with the promise of higher grade point averages on their transcripts. So a student earning an A in an AP course would be awarded a 5.0 for that course instead of a 4.0, and a B would equate to a 4.0 instead of 3.0, etc. Such increases in GPA would appeal to prospective colleges.

Thus began a new race, in which students competed for the treasured spots in prestigious Ivy League schools (Harvard, Yale, Stanford, and the like) or top-rated private colleges (such as University of California at Berkeley, University of Virginia, or University of Michigan).

Students then wanted to enroll in more than one AP (or IB or honors) course in order to earn that 5.0. They might take two, three, four, or even more AP courses in a given year, beginning as early as ninth grade. They might conclude their high school years with overall GPAs of 4.25, 4.4, or even 4.8.

At the end of these classes, tests are administered to determine the degree of student learning that took place. Students who scored well enough might be awarded college credit (and, in theory, reduce the time spent in core classes or in completing degrees, saving money and precious time down the road).

There are some strengths and numerous weaknesses in this approach. On the positive side, there is theoretically a higher amount of rigor attached to these courses. The material presented is of much greater depth and breadth. The students are challenged to compete with other motivated students and become better prepared to compete at the college level.

However, there can some significant drawbacks, which often are overlooked. The material in these classes consists of massive memorization of data (and because of greater breadth of the curriculum, this data is condensed into smaller segments of time). The courses lack real depth, even though the College Board is attempting to modify this component. The amount of content that is supposed to be covered is voluminous. To accomplish the degree of coverage requires accompanying amounts of homework, sometimes up to two hours per class, per day. If the students enroll in three or more courses, they could easily end up with three to five hours of homework per night. And, that amount of homework often conflicts with extracurricular activities such as sports, band, or theater that the students engage in and want to place on their resumes to appeal to the top schools, not to mention jobs, which may be a necessity for some students.

These classes lack the level of engagement and activities that would be possible were they just honors courses, because they come with the added pressure of being on target when the end-of-year exams arrive. In many cases, the high numbers of students enrolled in the AP-level courses only serve to weaken the rigor rather than increase it. If two hundred students are enrolled in an AP course—let's say AP English—out of a senior class of six hundred, and one teacher is carrying the full load, it is not likely that he/she can properly assign and evaluate the quantity of written work these students should complete.

All students deserve to be challenged. They deserve to be enrolled in classes where good teaching, resources, and technology are included to provide them with the tools needed to succeed in the next chapter of their lives, college or a vocation.

However, students also need to be part of an inclusive classroom environment and learn from all levels of other students. Also, they need to learn to maintain a balanced life, one whereby students learn how to study *and* play. Taking on a heavy load of Advanced Placement classes for the purpose of raising your GPA, then being force fed quantities of information, is not the way to achieve that balance.

ESSAY 28:

EDUCATION SWEEPSTAKES: WILL YOU BUY A TICKET?

Imagine that you won the lottery. What would you do with your winnings? And not just any lottery, but the big one, El Gordo, Powerball, or Mega on a high jackpot day. Maybe $25 million to $50 million in a lump sum, after taxes. C'mon, what would you really do? Buy a luxury jet? A mansion in the Hamptons? Produce your own version of a Kardashian reality show, starring yourself?

Well, first of all, we know that the odds of winning are ridiculous to begin with—about 175 million to one. And that's only if you choose to buy a ticket. There is an oft-cited statistic that the likelihood of your FINDING a million dollars is greater than that of your actually winning the lottery. But just for the sake of discussion, let's suppose you won. What would you do with all of that money?

As I've said many times in this column, education is the key ingredient for both the development of the individual and society at large. It is a win-win for everyone. And, since most of a child's brain development takes place before the age of three and definitely by the age of five, the earlier the better. Even kindergarten is often too late for students to begin to catch up.

So here is my plan, should my lucky numbers be drawn.

First, I would lay out my objective: Get all children up to age five access and exposure to early literacy and proper health. Of course, that would mean doing the same for their parents as well, because if the parents are illiterate and unhealthy, it's almost impossible to ensure that their children are able to overcome those characteristics long term.

Next, I would need to create a plan to make sure that this endeavor is regular and ongoing, not just a one-shot-and-done deal. Giving each baby's family a book at birth or reading to school children once a year for a community service project just so we can pat ourselves on the back won't cut it.

Also, this endeavor must be brought directly to the affected segments of the population. Just offering health services or free libraries is not enough. The individuals that need these services are not likely to just go get them. Often, they lack not only transportation but also understanding of the procedures required, usually because of a lack of information, lack of understanding English, or lack of experience. These services should be delivered.

In addition, many segments of the community should be involved, including health care professionals, representatives from social services, educators, elected officials, nonprofit groups, peace officers, and more. As a matter of fact, since this is a community issue affecting the entire community in some way, all groups should fill a role.

So, back to my plan. At least the big idea.

If I won the big one, I would purchase a fleet of specially designed buses or trailers. These vehicles would be divided into sections. One section would contain a mini-library/day-care center outfitted with materials for infant and toddler use. Another section would encompass a Wi-Fi center with laptops to teach literacy, technology, parenting, and job skills. A third section would offer health and social services to both parents and children.

These vehicles would have established routes throughout the city, something like a school bookmobile, targeting those areas most affected by poverty, poor health, and lack of parent education. Maybe they could stop for three hours in the morning and another three in the afternoon, moving to another neighborhood along the route the next day.

So the group would need to coordinate its objectives, as well as how best to market the program to the communities being served. Also, that group would need to gather together personnel to carry out the operation, which might include doctors, nurses, and social workers, as well as dentists, optometrists, or other health care professionals, all donating work pro bono. Possibly, we could connect to students in training, to provide on-the-job experience.

The same could be true with the education component. College or university personnel and students in teacher-training programs could man the preschool, technology, and parent literacy sections. Law enforcement organizations could have a presence as well. They could not only provide safety and security, but they could help establish additional positive connections to underserved neighborhoods.

Since the dream of my winning the state lottery is darn near impossible, let's frame it another way. If we all—individuals, businesses, and nonprofit organizations—invest in education through a contribution of resources, it would be like purchasing a ticket to the education lottery, and we can all share in the winnings.

I like those odds much better.

ESSAY 29:

DICHOTOMY OF TODAY'S
TEACHING AND LEARNING

Schools are in the business of educating students, and they operate on the principle that all students can and must learn.

This reflects a belief that education is not only important, but it is mandatory. If society requires that individuals and institutions be equipped to improve our political, economic, and social fabric, then an educated citizenry is essential.

However, in way too many instances in education today, there seems to be a system in place that runs counter to this goal, with rules and procedures that appear designed to oppose those objectives—a dichotomy. Speaking out of both sides of the mouth at the same time.

Numerous examples serve to illustrate this point.

Recent research, which has been documented for years, points out that students, especially teens, should not begin school until at least eight-thirty a.m. Their internal clocks run on different schedules than those of adults. They may not become tired until eleven p.m. or midnight. Teenagers also require more sleep than adults in order to function properly—about nine hours a night. This is a scientific fact.

Yet, a majority of schools begin their day around seven or eight a.m. The early start times are in place to facilitate parents' work schedules, bus transportation, or after-school activities, such as athletics.

But the deeper point is that students are losing sleep, which is not only unhealthy but also leaves them physically and mentally unprepared for learning.

Several other examples of this dichotomy relate to numbers. Students should be given enough personal attention to facilitate learning the necessary content, processes, or skills. However, many classrooms contain thirty or forty students at a time, even in the primary grades, without additional paraprofessionals. Are those ratios going to enable the teacher to provide for the individual needs of their students? Effective teachers may be able to manage these size classes, but ensuring individual attention? Not likely.

School enrollments are another issue. The most appropriate school size for high schools, to maximize student learning in relation to education need, is in the range of 650 to 850 students. However, many high schools number in the range of 2,000 to 3,000 students per school, sometimes even more. In years past, a factory model might have served a purpose—for instance, training students to work on an assembly line. Today, though, students must develop critical thinking, interpersonal communication, and technological skills, whether or not they choose to enroll in four-year universities. Enrollments this high create disconnection not only among students but also among students and teachers, counselors, and administrators. Correcting this issue requires money, but as a society, are we willing to pay to address this dichotomy, or is the status quo good enough?

Also, in the area of teaching, some polar opposites exist. As far as the role that schools can play, teachers have been shown to be the single most important ingredient in the education of students. But, in too many instances, they are not provided with the assistance and support necessary to be successful. This is particularly noticeable among beginning teachers and those teachers who are struggling. If the educational system truly believes that all can and must learn, then supporting teachers is necessary in order to make this happen.

In addition, the most talented teachers should be assigned the most challenging or underperforming students. Yet often the best teachers are scheduled into the most advanced classes. Or those with the most seniority are allowed to choose their schedules— perhaps remaining in the same grade level for thirty years or teaching five classes of the same subject—whereas new teachers might be assigned the more rigorous load. This dichotomy runs counterproductive to the expressed goal of providing students with the most effective learning environment.

A similar contrast is found in the roles of both administrators and unions. The vast majority of teachers do a fantastic job in a challenging profession. However, a minority of teachers simply are not meant to remain in this career. Administrators and unions are both complicit in this situation. Administrators have the right to dismiss teachers within their probationary periods, usually the first two or three years. Too many times, however, they let such individuals remain in their jobs, which in effect denies students access to good teaching.

The same is true for unions. While they do serve as a necessary bulwark in protecting teachers against an onslaught of parents, incompetent administrators, and excessive rules and regulations, they also act as a barrier against removing incompetent teachers. Again, though the primary objective for schools is to provide for the effective education of students, their goal will never be achieved with lazy or ineffective instructors. Pulling in opposite directions achieves nothing.

Schools and society cannot have it both ways. Are schools, taxpayers, and government leaders trying to please parents, teachers, and business offices? Or is the goal to provide the best education for the students? This dichotomy only serves to exacerbate the struggle to provide solutions to our educational challenges.

ESSAY 30:

STEEP LEARNING CURVE FOR NEW TEACHERS

You've heard the term "herding cats," but have you ever tried juggling cats? Try to imagine that concept. You take one cat and throw up it into the air, then add a second, then a third. Pretty soon, if you even get that far, you are going to get scratched and probably drop one. Tough job for both the juggler and the cats, but at least cats land on their feet. In schools, new teachers are essentially trying to do the same thing, except that they have never learned how to juggle.

If our goal is to improve our future way of life, then we need students to survive and thrive. To accomplish that, we need new teachers who are up to the task. They need to learn how to juggle.

Beginning teachers, for several reasons, are so overwhelmed by juggling the numerous tasks required of them that it often takes years for them to "get it." Of course, many new teachers cannot juggle at all, or the stress of trying to do so results in approximately half of all new teachers leaving the profession within five years. We cannot allow this scenario to continue.

The two biggest issues new teachers face include classroom management and understanding of material.

Because we have such a diverse population in schools today, the expression of respect, appropriate behavior toward rules and procedures, proper treatment of others, and even good manners may not have been cultivated in the student's home environment. Those conditions serve to make classroom management difficult.

New teachers are in the midst of developing relationships with their students, creating their own rules and procedures and methods for enforcing them, and trying to establish the most effective tone for addressing challenges that arise. Students are not necessarily bad, but they do know how to smell blood in the water, and the new teachers are fresh meat.

Often, non-teachers assume that teachers have a clear grasp of the material and resources that are being presented. Generally, that is far from the reality. Elementary teachers might have credentials for teaching multiple subjects, but their student teaching experiences and interests may have been in grades one, two, and three, while they may have been hired to teach sixth grade, which has vastly different needs. A high school teacher may have acquired a degree in American history and completed student teaching in grades seven and eight, yet his or her job may call for teaching American government and economics to twelfth-grade students—totally different material and students.

In addition to developing relationships, rules, and procedures and trying to learn the course material, unless they want to read a script all day, teachers need to acquire or create materials and activities on the fly.

The challenge, of course, is to teach the required curriculum and to engage the students in learning. However, accomplishing that requires understanding and experience, both of which new teachers lack. Also, in today's educational setting, students frequently lack skills and prior knowledge of content, which impedes the new teacher's ability to make connections to class material.

Besides these areas, new teachers have to learn the applicable technology, comprehend district and school policies, attend professional development meetings, develop effective communication strategies with parents, and, above all, correct mountains of paperwork. In other words, juggle cats.

To attempt to combat these difficulties, schools should be more effective in supporting new teachers as they learn how to manage their many tasks and minimize their tunnel vision in order to utilize so many skills at once.

First off, new teachers should have reduced workloads—not to make their lives easy, but to allow them some time to assimilate the overwhelming stress confronting them. Yes, the profession is one of joy and the rewards of making a difference, but not if you drown before discovering those experiences. Instead of having new elementary teachers teaching full time in their first year, perhaps they should work partial school days. For high school teachers, instead of requiring them to teach two or three different subjects over a five-period day, why not have them teach four periods of one subject? Their out-of-class time can be spent developing resources and observing other teachers—just getting a handle on the profession.

Also, new teachers need mentors or coaches—full-time partners who not only who help them fill out forms or provide ideas for activities here and there, but also who can share observations of classes, help reflect on past experiences, discuss particular students' circumstances, and share ideas.

In addition, schools should assist in developing more comprehensive classroom volunteer programs, especially in elementary schools. More help is needed from volunteers who can assist in making copies, grading papers, organizing materials, or even working with individuals or small groups of students.

There is a tremendous shortage of teachers. Significant numbers of those who do become teachers move on to other professions. In order for us to achieve the ultimate goal—producing educated, motivated, and thoughtful students—we need to take more care in developing our teachers. Helping them learn to effectively juggle these tasks and their students' needs will help all of us land on our feet.

ESSAY 31:

TEACHER LEARNING BUILT
ON ACCEPTANCE

"Could a greater miracle take place than for us to look through each other's eyes for an instant?"
~ Henry David Thoreau, from *Walden*

Teachers, more than those in almost any other profession, have opportunities to practice the meaning of Thoreau's words every day. Teachers hear their students' voices and know of their experiences. They more vividly see their students' lives and their many challenges than those who taught decades ago.

When any person first enters a chosen profession, that person brings along his or her own biases and stereotypes. For teachers, this is especially important to understand due to the extensively varied makeup of today's student body.

So when a student enters a classroom with ten-inch spiked hair and numerous piercings, there may be a tendency on the teacher's part to make a judgment. When a third-grade student shows up to class a month after the school year has begun, accompanied by parents who do not speak English, a teacher may tend to make a judgment. And when a student comes in on the first day of class with sagging pants and pounding rap music reverberating from his headphones, a similar type of judgment may occur.

However, after getting to know students as individuals and establishing rapport with them, a teacher gains insight into the real people behind these student personas and can recognize their uniqueness as individuals, not as stereotypes. Such students can turn out to be very respectful and responsible. Mr. Spiked Hair may be a solid student who hopes to become a computer graphics designer. Our third-grader could wind up being the highest-performing student in the class and a teacher favorite. And Mr. Saggy Pants might become a county honor band trumpet player.

Good teachers learn to see beyond the stereotypes and find the people underneath them.

Of course, there are those individuals who, on first glance, seem to fit the mold of compliant, capable, and hard-working students, only to end up regularly missing class, failing to complete work, and disrupting others when they are present. However, teachers need to learn to deal with these behaviors as they occur and not base actions on preconceived biases. It can be a challenge.

Another opportunity afforded teachers, especially those who establish early relationships and learn to listen to students, is that of hearing students' real stories, the pieces that make up their inner selves.

I recall an instance when I was teaching a class of ninth-grade students. In the middle of the year, three additional students, siblings from Cambodia, were admitted. This was prior to the advent of separate English Language Learner classes. None of the three could speak English. In the newspaper, shortly after their arrival, was an article that I read to my class about a family of refugees fleeing the Khmer Rouge. It described their forced marches through the jungle, their lack of food and clothing, the murder of their father, and the six months they spent in camps in Thailand. As it turned out, those were the very students sitting in my class. It was an eye-opening experience for my students and myself. These siblings became comfortable sharing their story with me and ended up being wonderful, hardworking individuals who successfully graduated when their four years were completed.

Teachers are confronted with endlessly challenging scenarios from their students on an almost daily basis. One might be an elementary student who lives with an aged grandmother in an overcrowded apartment as a result of parents being in the throes of drug abuse or in prison. Or one could be a student who is dealing with significant health disorders, such as anorexia, anxiety, or stress, while the parents are unaware or don't know how to effectively deal with it. One might be a homosexual student who comes out to his/her parents and is subsequently kicked out of the home. And another might be a student who develops leukemia and has to undergo treatment, which creates significant repercussions while the student is trying to maintain grades.

These and other instances students face—poverty, physical and sexual abuse, bullying, and substance use—present challenges not only for the students and their families, but for teachers as well. Students often reveal themselves to teachers in unusual or interesting ways. The manner in which a teacher accepts the individual determines the teacher's ability to offer direction and assistance. These situations enable, and in fact require, teachers to provide resources for the students and their families such as counseling services, social welfare organizations, or law enforcement.

Students today reflect the ongoing changes that confront society as a whole. The issues of immigration, gangs, income gaps, and racial conflicts all become abundantly clear in a school environment. Teachers, by being attentive listeners and establishing positive relationships with their students, can place themselves in positions of tremendous influence on those students' lives and the choices they make.

The ongoing exposure teachers have to their students—listening to them and interacting with them daily—also provides them with opportunities to become learners themselves. They can develop greater degrees of caring, compassion, tolerance, and patience both within their profession and in their lives outside of school.

One never knows where a genius may be found or how a teacher's impact may be felt. Only time and distance will tell for sure, but acceptance now is more likely to reap those benefits in the future.

ESSAY 32:

KEEPING EYES ON THE PRIZE

It's a phrase we hear all the time, but historically speaking, the term *Eyes on the Prize* was the name of a folk song from the 1950s and '60s that became influential during the American Civil Rights movement. It later became the name of a 1987 PBS documentary about the Civil Rights movement in the United States. The goal, or prize, was the achievement of equal rights, specifically for African Americans, and the phrase meant to continue the struggle until this goal was reached.

However, that phrase continues to remain relevant, not only for African American children, but for all children in our educational system. The number of bureaucratic initiatives proposed by state and national governments has become a maze of policies and programs that blur the goal of equal education.

In addition, the congested web of local administrative rules and procedures handed down from county offices of education to school boards, school superintendents, and district administrators has created the impression that goals are being reached.

In reality, the only true goal, the true prize, is the improvement of teachers' ability to teach and students to learn at the classroom level. That is being compromised by all the gobbledygook.

Change is afoot, by way of the school reform movement, and these changes are not all necessarily bad. However, they produce extensive quantities of bureaucratic hoops that principals and teachers have to jump through. This takes away time, energy, and resources that would be better served where they are most needed: the classroom.

There are now state content standards and national performance standards in place. There are attempts to refocus teaching on employing the Common Core standards and to alter the scripted style of teaching from past decades, which included completely teacher-directed instruction. There are new methods of assessment as well, with many states using the Smarter Balance test and some states using alternate tests. Also, there is renewed emphasis on STEM (Science, Technology, Engineering, Mathematics) programs and career education. New funding formulas in many states allow districts to make decisions on how to allocate resources. The use of technology in the classroom is expanding, and there is talk about teaching to the whole child, meaning not just drilling content into a student's head, but addressing that student's physical, mental, and emotional needs as well.

Change is necessary and useful, but only if the result is better teaching and learning.

In too many classrooms, teachers are so overwhelmed by the day-to-day operations of preparing lessons, controlling behavior, addressing significant learning deficiencies, and dealing with parents that they cannot focus on their primary responsibility: teaching students.

As with everything, education must build upon fundamentals. Should schools have standards? Absolutely. They should also have rigor. However, the makeup of the classroom ought to give teachers and students a chance at success. If the rooms are overcrowded and include significant numbers of students who by third grade still can't count by tens or read at a kindergarten level, it is time to back up.

Classroom assessment, too, is critical, but to require students in kindergarten, first, or even second grade to complete computerized district or state assessments several times a year is to lose sight of the goal.

Also, technology is a fantastic tool, but only when used in spurts. If fully implemented, it does require significant chunks of time during each day. Students need to learn the fundamentals of focus, paying attention to the teacher, communicating with peers, and participating in whole-class communication. Those skills can be developed along with technological implementation, but technology should not supplant that development.

Emphasis must be placed on providing the greatest resources to those schools/teachers/students that face the greatest needs. As research has shown, and as I have mentioned previously, if students are not performing at grade level by the end of third grade, their chances of graduating from high school dramatically decrease.

In schools where the students are already succeeding, generally those from higher income families with more highly educated parents, less modification may be called for.

However, in districts and schools with the neediest students—often the poorest or least educated and least language proficient—adjustments should be made to target their needs. We need to reduce the top-down massive stumbling blocks that create barriers to providing what the teachers and students need.

More teachers, especially more experienced teachers, ought to be placed in those low-performing schools, and class sizes must be greatly reduced. Permanent classroom assistants should be hired, additional counselors and specialists employed, and preschool and early childhood programs expanded.

In addition, parental communication and education must be significantly enhanced. The job of teachers and schools is NOT to raise children but to educate them. When children come to school with diminished social skills, manners, and respect for others (including the teacher), educating them often becomes near impossible. If we want educated students, we must put more emphasis on partnering with parents to better understand their circumstances and to support them as they take responsibility for necessary for raising mature, conscientious children. What doesn't help are additional bureaucratic mandates, whether from the national, state, or district level.

The prize that can result from these changes is children who are prepared to be responsible, productive, contributing citizens in a democracy. This can only happen if we focus our eyes on the target, the students in the classroom.

ESSAY 33:

CONNECTING THE DOTS

The purpose of learning is not just to be able to recall terms, equations, formulas, or dates. In fact, as students matriculate from elementary school, middle school, and high school, the emphasis on the rote recall of information is a major reason students often turn off to learning.

All students, young or old, need to comprehend the basics in reading, math, and writing. Schools and parents must work to ensure that students acquire mastery of the fundamentals. However, after a certain point in their learning, students do not need to participate in the incessant recall of minutia in order to be considered educated.

"So what?" is a question that not only students should be asking; teachers and everyone else who is involved educating children should be asking it, too.

Connections are what matter. Connections are the keys that unlock the meaning and value of learning. Teachers must emphasize why one piece of knowledge or one concept or one discipline is connected to another. Students should understand why something matters besides how it will affect their scores on tests.

For example, consider the following questions:

What significance does Shakespeare's *Romeo and Juliet* have for today's students?

How is the situation (any situation) in the Middle East relevant?

What is causing the demise of coral reefs?

Why is radiation or chemotherapy employed to treat cancers?

Do questions such as these connect? And in what ways do they have significance to students' lives?

The integration of lessons, assignments, and activities that promote thinking should be the real purpose of education.

The prior knowledge that students bring with them into learning situations are of great importance in building those connections. However, with the tremendous levels of poverty in our country today, the differences in culture, language, and family income often preclude the acquisition of knowledge on a variety of course subjects. Students also lack significant shared experiences upon which this knowledge can build.

With my students, I always attempted to employ the use of SSC: self, school, and community. All of the students have that much in common. If I can break down an issue or topic into examples that students can connect to SSC, then I have a place to start and upon which to build.

Then, as a teacher, I can use that now-shared knowledge to tie the course content to their life experiences and help them answer "So what?" and make learning meaningful.

As to the questions posed above, they all have to do with conflicts—between families, religions, environmental organisms, or chemical reactions. One side attacks, the other defends or counterattacks in an effort to survive. So, then, let's teach about conflict and use the world of the students to connect to the larger themes.

Over the past fifteen or twenty years, the emphasis in education reform has been on stuffing content into students' heads and requiring them to regurgitate that material on standardized tests. Then they and their schools are judged on those results. That information really does not prove students have knowledge or can apply it to actual situations.

Think about it. When does a person really need to know the name of the guy whose assassination led to WWI or the quadratic formula or the chemicals in the periodic table or the soliloquy of Hamlet? If you are a contestant on *Jeopardy*, sure, but in normal daily life? It's not likely.

But if a teacher can connect that information to big concepts such as equality (math, chemistry, history); change (biology, music, English, government); or perspective (art, English, history, foreign language), to name just a few, the students can begin to make sense of the material and see the value of education, and maybe even get excited about learning.

In addition, through discussions, activities, and projects, the opportunities students have to integrate their prior knowledge can also assist in the development of individual and class character. Soft skills, such as listening, tolerance, reflection, verbal communication, even manners and respect, can be promoted.

Course content by itself does have value, but not as much as the students' ability to understand and apply that content.

As students move on from high school to either college or the world of work, if they possess the ability to see connections and apply experiences to action, work with others, and make sense of the world around them, these things will prove assets to both themselves and society at large. Universities or employers can train people in the specifics of a course or a project.

Well, that is the point of school. The connections students can make between content and process, present and past, and the world of school and the world of life can also foster a quest for a pursuit of knowledge. That is a lesson to learn.

APPENDIX:

Effective Reading Strategies
for Accessing Informational Texts
A Top Twenty-two

Research has demonstrated that literacy remains the key ingredient to improving student understanding and performance. That improvement in literacy needs to occur not just in English classes, but also in content areas across the curriculum, especially with today's Common Core emphasis on informational texts. Whether the reading is a textbook, novel, speech, current event piece, or primary source article, effective processing of the content will enhance student comprehension. I have developed a collection of successful strategies, which I call "a Top Twenty-two" to assist teachers in making any reading assignment effective and engaging.

These strategies are meant to serve as guides for teachers and students alike. A benefit of each strategy is that it may be done independently or in pairs or small groups. Also, they all involve student choice and encourage different ways for students to examine an issue. In addition, the teacher may decide to allow short paragraph responses or more in-depth analyses.

Note: In these strategies, I have not included actual diagrams of how I use them. I want teachers to learn to process the strategies themselves in order to internalize their own understanding.

Extra, extra! Read all about it! Students read an article or small section of text, brainstorm important information, and then develop newspaper stories using their own words to process meaning for increased understanding. Included must be a headline, lead sentence, and important details. They will have an opportunity to share this story with other students, who may have read the same piece of text or a connected one.

The photo shop: Students are assigned a section of reading. From that reading, they are to create X number of pictures or symbols (often four to eight) that represent their selection of the key points from that section. The pictures may be created on white paper, with one, two, or even four visuals per page. On the reverse side of the paper, students briefly describe the name of the idea, event, or concept in each, and the reason they felt it should be included. Upon returning to class, students can discuss their work in groups with other students who read the same sections, to reinforce the main points of each section, or with a cross-section of students who read other sections, in order to gain a broader sense of material. Teachers can incorporate ways to assist students in developing overview connections of the key concepts.

What's in a name? Students are assigned to read a section or chapter. As they read, they are to develop a poem-type processing work by paraphrasing content which lends meaning to a particular concept being studied in class (i.e. progressivism, evolution, metamorphosis, tolerance, etc.). The selected term is placed top to bottom on the left margin of the page. For instance, take the term *genocide*. The letters G-E-N-O-C-I-D-E would be written vertically down the left side of the page. Next to the

G, a student might write "Germany applied this concept to the Jews during WWII," and for E, he or she might write, "Engaged and applied by totalitarian forms of government," and so forth. They continue down the letters of the word in order to form some acquired meaning of the concept obtained from their reading.

Answer the question! Students often face content in text format that features numerous headings and subheadings. To assist students in making meaning for each section, teachers can train students to convert the headings into questions that they develop. From there, they can read the section that follows each and answer the question by paraphrasing the information contained in the section.

Chicken or egg? Teachers assign students a series of paired items from a reading. The students' task is to first read the selection and briefly define each pair of items. Next, the students have to indicate which item occurred first and describe why they have answered this way.

Pick a side, any side: If a section of reading contains two points of view, two main characters, two arguments or perspectives, etc., students can develop a T chart in which the two sides, viewpoints, etc. are written side by side across the top of the "T," and a vertical line goes down the center of the page, dividing it into two columns, one for each side. Then students begin listing the main points from each. Then, below the chart, ask the students to formulate their own opinions as to which side contains the most merit and why.

The yellow brick road: Usually, in a section of reading, a series of events or actions takes the reader from the introduction to the conclusion. The teacher can provide the students with a beginning point and an ending point, and the students need to identify X number of points along the logical path from beginning to end. Afterward, they can be asked to make judgments as to which points were the most important and why.

What happened, and what would have happened if this hadn't happened? Teachers can assign students selected items from a section of reading. There could be historical events, character plots, lab results, etc. that the students are supposed to describe. After each description, the students could create potential scenarios showing what possible results might have occurred if the original item had never occurred.

Connect the dots: The teacher selects a series of key vocabulary words, events, personalities, etc. from a section of material. Students are assigned the task of connecting one item with another and explaining the connection.

Scrabble with 5 Ws and an H: In this strategy, teachers use a more specific brainstorm guide to have students examine a particular event or action. First, the teacher selects a particular event and assigns a student or group of students to uncover this event. The students, using a blank piece of paper, place the name of the event on the center of the page. Next, around the outside of the paper, students write the who, what, when, where, why, and how of the event. As students or groups read a section, they place the appropriate information from the article onto the paper. This can then be shared with the class or a group in the class by way of a jigsaw strategy.

Conversation piece: This strategy can be effective when trying to have students understand the thinking of an individual character. After reading a section of work, particularly biographical sketches, poetry, or plays, students can either develop or be assigned questions or scenarios to respond to through the eyes of a character. This may be done individually or in pairs. Also, it may be conducted through a T chart when comparing two separate individuals.

Pyramid engineering: In order to promote students' thinking about the big ideas contained within a particular piece of work, they can be assigned a layered pyramid to fill in. On the top layer might be the big idea that's central to the reading or even beyond the reading. On the next layer, the various topics that are discussed within that article can be described, followed by details listed in the final layer.

Prove it: Acting as lawyers or detectives, students can be assigned the task of uncovering the clues to an argument or conclusion. The teacher can pose a hypothesis and ask the students individually, in pairs, or in small groups to read the information, identifying any evidence that would prove or disprove the hypothesis.

Topical triangulation: Students often have difficulty connecting disparate information around a common theme. To assist this understanding, teachers can assign students groups of three words (terms, events, people, vocabulary, dates, etc.).

The task is to use a triangle formation on a piece of paper (or half of one), placing each of the three words at an apex. First, define each word itself, and then, in the center of the triangle, write a paragraph that explains the connections between the three words, to demonstrate understanding.

Puzzle maker: Students can be given a large series of words from a reading to be completed. As they read the article or section of reading, they have to place the words into their proper chronological order and explain their relationships. Different explanations can be shared and discussed with the whole class.

Read it backward and wonder why: To promote inquiry, students can be asked to read a particular article, text section, or chapter from back to front. As they complete each part, they need to ask one or two questions about what might have happened to lead up to this point or conclusion. As they continue to read, they can answer their questions and pose others.

I found it! For this strategy, students are assigned to read a powerful nonacademic article and select meaningful words or phrases, then read them as a found poem—again, to allow creativity or increase understanding. The students may place these found words into a rap style if they so choose.

Mr. Postman: Students are asked to read a portion of an article and write down particular conditions or arguments that are presented. Next, they are instructed on the process of writing a letter. Their task is to compose a letter to a character related to the reading's content.

Word! To promote vocabulary understanding, students are provided with a series of terms (say ten) from an article or section to be read. Their task is to read the article until they come to the first word. When they locate the word, on a piece of paper they should identify the word, define it by way of dictionary, paraphrase it with regard to the reading, and describe its connection to the content.

Before and after: In this strategy, teachers employ a guided prereading for development of understanding. Teachers distribute a collection of several pictures, titles, graphs, charts, or cartoons from the reading to each student or pair. Students are taught how to decipher the information from the visuals and make a list of the acquired information on the left side of a divided piece of paper. Next, students are assigned the actual text section to read. Upon return, students are provided with the same collection of visuals again. This time, however, students are asked to add newly acquired descriptions and details related to the visuals to demonstrate enhanced understanding. Class discussion can follow to elaborate.

Sort of: To promote the skill of categorizing as well as making meaning, students can be assigned a particular reading segment. After completing the reading, they are handed a sheet of paper with a large assortment of words (key terms, events, people, vocabulary, dates, etc.). Individually or in small groups, the students are to pull out groups of three to five items that they feel fit together. They have to prepare explanations for how or why the words connect. Terms may be used in more than one connection pattern. One group could even compete against another in a contest.

Caught in the middle: Many times, students have difficulty understanding how an idea, event, or action that they are reading about or studying in class fits in with the actions going on around it. In this strategy, students select or can be provided with certain information (e.g. an event, concept, action). Their task is to place the items, spaced vertically in the middle of a clean sheet of paper. On the left of the item, they are to list possible causes, precursors, or reasons for the rise or onset of each item. On the right, students are to describe actions, consequences, or steps that resulted from that particular item.

ACKNOWLEDGEMENTS

I would like to thank some individuals for their assistance in this endeavor. First, my wife of forty-one years, Cheryl, deserves my enduring love for patiently discussing my incessant ideas for new articles, and for her guidance through the use of tactful suggestions. Also, I would like to thank my neighbor, Martha Hanyak, whose effective use of her red pen enabled me to sound somewhat literate in my written expression. Finally, I would like to thank the thousands of students and teachers I have had the pleasure to work with over the decades. Their willingness to face the hard challenges involved in promoting the educated person and fostering the next generation of leaders in our society is truly inspiring.

ABOUT THE AUTHOR

Larry White taught for thirty-four years at Lincoln High School in Stockton, California. His main areas of instruction were American government, United States history, world history, and economics. During this time, he also instructed new teachers and served as a visiting educator on loan to the San Joaquin County Office of Education. In addition, he served as Social Science Department chairman, mentor teacher, and master teacher at Lincoln High School, and he supervised student teachers for the University of the Pacific. Also, he worked with students of all ability levels, from Advanced Placement to at-risk youth, through a program he helped establish called the Academic Success Center.

Upon retirement, Larry began volunteering his time as an aide to primary grade students and working with a local Rotary club's literacy program to provide books and readers to low-performing schools.

Larry currently resides in Stockton with wife, Cheryl. He is the father of three grown children and has one beautiful granddaughter, Kaia.

Follow Larry White's work on:
Facebook — larrywhiteeducation
Twitter — @larrywhiteeducation
Instagram — @larrywhiteeducation